D0523051

Yum-Yum Bento All Year Round

Copyright © 2016 by Crystal Watanabe and Maki Ogawa

All rights reserved. Except as authorized under U.S. copyright law, no part of this book may be reproduced in any form without written permission from the publisher.

Library of Congress Cataloging in Publication Number: 2016930955

ISBN: 978-1-59474-938-4

Printed in China

Typeset in Helvetica Rounded and Century Schoolbook

Photography by Maki Ogawa
Designed by Katie Hatz
Production management by John J. McGurk

Quirk Books
215 Church Street
Philadelphia, PA 19106

quirkbooks.com

10 9 8 7 6 5 4 3 2 1

Yum-Yum Bento
All Year Round

Box Lunches for Every Season

By Crystal Watanabe and Maki Ogawa

QUIRK BOOKS

PHILADELPHIA

Contents

I'm hungry right meow!

Hello Again from Maki and Pikko

Aloha, bento friends! Konnichiwa, cute charaben fans! We are delighted to be back for a sequel to *Yum-Yum Bento Box: Fresh Recipes for Adorable Lunches*. Once an obscure culinary hobby outside Japan, bento is now a trend around the world. If you're new to it, we hope this book will be not only a source of inspiration for yummy foods and cute character ideas, but also a lesson in creating art with edible ingredients.

Bento-making can be a rewarding experience, particularly now that sharing images on social media is so easy. Even though we've been making bento for years, we are still learning new techniques and ways to be creative. We learn by seeing other bento works, making friends, asking questions, and adding our own spin to others' ideas.

Since we first published *Yum-Yum Bento Box* in 2010, our little children have grown into preteens and teens, but our families' love for our bento still prevails. A ten-year-old son still requests the Sports Bento. A twelve-year-old daughter shows her kawaii lunch to her middle-school friends. A two-year-old son will soon find himself the subject of many test recipes and charaben. Even without the cutesy characters, these lunches are well-balanced and visually appealing meals

that will delight people of any age.

The bento boxes in this book are divided into seasons—Springtime Fun for spring showers and the reemergence of flowers, Summertime Splash for the hot and sunny months, Fall Frenzy for turning leaves and autumn holidays, and Winter Wonderland for the chilly days when delicious food and smiles make the cold easier to tolerate.

We hope you will have a wonderful time making and sharing our cute obento designs throughout the year—and for years to come!

My friends and I are here to help you out!

Getting Started

Before you dig in, here are some of the tools, skills, and ingredients you'll want to pack into your bento toolbox. With practice and a little inspiration, you'll be ready to start your adorable adventure!

Tools for All Seasons

Although special cutters and sandwich presses make bento easy, you may find your kitchen (and your home!) overrun with these items if you're not careful. Here are some of the tools and accessories we use most often.

An **insulated bento box set** has a container in which to keep food warm, along with two smaller side dish containers. Take it to school or work in a matching tote bag to express your individual style.

Wooden bento boxes, or *mage wappa*, have a traditional, sleek style. Cedar boxes in particular have a wonderful aroma. To prevent staining, line your box with waxed or parchment paper before filling it.

Plastic bento boxes with domed lids are best for charaben because they cover the bento without smashing and ruining your hard work.

Metal bento boxes are great for overeager children who have a tendency to break plastic ones, and they come in a variety of ecofriendly and easy-to-maintain options.

Mini ice packs are invaluable for keeping your bento cool until lunchtime.

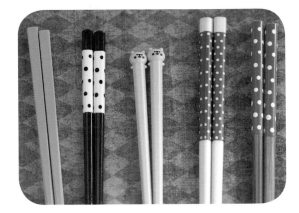

Silicone cups are great for holding small portions of "wet" salads, like those dressed with mayonnaise or containing fruit—plus they're reusable. Paper cups are better for holding fried foods.

Sauce bottles and cups are a great way to pack a small serving of sauce. Another option is to save packets of soy sauce, ketchup, and tonkatsu sauce from take-out restaurants.

Don't quite have the hang of **chopsticks** yet? Using them to make bento is good practice. They're particularly handy for scrambling eggs, stir-frying, and arranging noodles or bite-sized pieces of food in a bento.

Kitchen shears serve many purposes in bento-making. For cutting tiny pieces of nori, a pair of **micro-tip scissors** is your best friend. Be sure to label your "nori scissors" to prevent crafty kiddos from borrowing them!

Nori or craft punches make easy work of creating cute character faces. Look for punches that have metal dies; plastic ones don't cut as well.

Food dividers, also known as *baran* or antibacterial sheets, are available in a wide variety of cute designs as well as the classic "sushi grass" style.

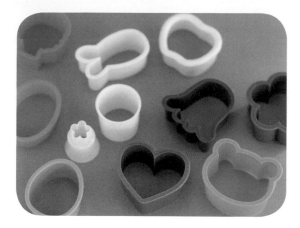

Drinking straws of various sizes are great for making small, round facial features. Cut them into 1-inch lengths so they last as long as possible.

Tweezers help you position tiny details cut from sheets of nori. Look for sets that have a bent end for ease of use.

Plastic food cutters are great for soft foods, but sets that cut out face shapes can be difficult to find a practical use for, and specially shaped cutters can fill up all the space in your drawers. Consider cutting your own specialty shapes with toothpicks.

Hand-held hole punchers are great for making lots of tiny dots at once. The standard and ⅛-inch sizes are our favorites be-cause they're just right for eyes and noses. If you can, find one with a rubber grip.

Mini food cutters, usually made out of metal, are great for cutting slices of carrot and potato to be used as garnishes and accents. Wash and dry them soon after use to prevent rusting and food build-up.

Toothpicks are a wonderful multifunctional, disposable tool. Use them to trace shapes, paint cheese, or apply the tiniest pieces of nori. Just dab the tip on a moist paper towel to pick the pieces up.

Rice paddles are used for mixing sushi rice, and miniature versions are great for flattening it. Paddles are made of bamboo or plastic; the plastic ones are specially coated so they don't stick to rice.

Tracing or parchment paper is an easy way to transfer designs from paper to food, such as cheese. Sometimes having a guide can make all the difference in creating just the right shape for your charaben.

Food picks are handy for securing foods and accenting rice balls. A set of hat picks can make a rabbit rice ball into an instant Rabbit King (crown) or Gentleman Rabbit (top hat).

Cute **sandwich cutters** are a quick way to make irresistibly adorable sandwiches. Just be sure to moisten the press with water to ensure the design imprints firmly into the bread slice.

Bamboo sushi mats are useful when you want to form maki sushi (rolled sushi) or shape tamagoyaki (rolled omelet) into a round or rectangle shape. They can also be used to drain soba or somen noodles for salads.

Got lots of leftover notebooks, pencils, crayons, and colored pencils from your child's school supplies at the end of the year? Use them to sketch bento ideas and cute characters.

Bento Packing Basics

All of the lunches in this book can be adjusted to make larger portions or omit the cute characters. Beneath all the fun and smiles are delicious recipes for people of all ages. Don't want cute cats smiling at you? Simply add plain boiled eggs sliced in half to a lunch.

The vast majority of these meals contain rice, which is the primary starch in Japan and Hawaii, where we live. That said, except for the rice ball recipes, you can always substitute other starches, such as mashed potatoes or cauliflower, quinoa, or pasta. Simply adapt our designs for your personal preferences. Get creative!

The basis for all of our bento designs is not the cute character, but the lunch it accompanies. Feel free to mix and match side dishes and characters, achieving almost the same effect. Here are some basic bento-packing tips to make lunch prep quick and easy.

Make characters in advance.

Nothing is more hectic than mornings in a house full of kids. Because you'll be chasing around for clothes to be put on, teeth to get brushed, and homework to be packed up (after they unpack it from the night before, of course), having your little quail-egg chunks or cute *kamaboko* doggies all ready to go in your fridge can be a lifesaver.

Store characters made with cheese on wax paper to prevent sticking and cover with plastic wrap. In the morning, discard the plastic and pack the characters into your bento.

Prep veggies the night before.

Packing a lunch with rice the night before and refrigerating it is not recommended, because the rice will dry out, but boiling and cutting your vegetables the night before is a useful and recommended time-saver. Wash and dry lettuce leaves and boil broccoli, carrot, and potato slices. Cut them into shapes, cover, and store.

Use up leftovers.

Don't have time to play short-order cook in the morning? Utilize leftovers by setting aside a small bento-sized portion from dinner in the evening. Mince leftover meats to stuff into rice balls or chop up for fried rice. Always try to pack lunches with fresh or reheated rice. To make refrigerated rice fluffy again, cover the rice with a moistened paper towel and microwave for a minute or so.

Make a bento palette.

The starch is usually the background for our bentos. We start most of our lunches by packing in a portion of rice, often enough to fill half the bento box, then flattening the top with a fork or mini rice paddle. Use the same utensil to straighten the edge of the rice to make space in the box for side dishes. If you're using a starch or protein that is a little too loose and may shift around, consider making a smooth egg omelet to contain it and create a palette for your cute character.

To create a smooth omelet, strain a beaten egg into a bowl to remove the lumps. In another bowl mix together a small amount of water and cornstarch, and then mix this slurry into the egg. Cook in a small pan over low heat until firm, adding food coloring or natural coloring ingredients if desired.

Line with lettuce leaves.

You'll notice that nearly all of our bentos contain lettuce leaves. The leaves serve multiple purposes. They help to keep foods separate, which is great when you don't want saucy foods to mix with rice or side dishes. Lettuce also provides a splash of color, which can instantly transform a dull yellow or brown bento into something dynamic and bright. Other wonderful leafy green options include mizuna, kale, purple kale, red leaf lettuce, and shingiku.

Include bento fillers.

An essential part of making your bento lunch look complete is filling in the open areas between your main dish and starch. Look at what's available in your market and pack what's in abundance. Are the Honeycrisps particularly good in a certain month? Cut some up for your bento! Are the strawberries sweeter from a certain roadside stand only during one particular time of the year? Use them instead of tomatoes! This will give your seasonal lunch an even fresher taste.

If you pack lunches for work, store a bottle of your favorite salad dressing in the office fridge and finish your lunch with a mini salad of leftover lettuce.

Natural Ways to Dye Rice

Colorful rice is an easy way to add a burst of personality to your bento. Cook the rice as usual, but add food coloring to the water. Or stir in food coloring to cooked rice while it's still hot. Start with a little of the coloring ingredient and add more as you stir until the rice becomes the color you want. The rice will be difficult to dye once it has cooled.

Although store-bought food coloring is a convenient way to achieve almost any color of rice, you don't have to dye rice artificially. Here are some of the colors you can create with natural ingredients.

Red

pickled ginger, minced (pictured)
red pepper, minced

Orange

finely grated carrot
ketchup (pictured)

Yellow

boiled egg yolk (pictured)
curry powder
mashed squash

Green

dried parsley
edamame, minced (pictured)
spinach powder

Blue

purple potato powder
decofuri (pictured)

Purple

mashed purple sweet potato
yukari or shiso fumi furikake (pictured)

Brown

soy sauce (pictured)
bonito flakes

Gray

black sesame seed powder (pictured)

Black

nori (pictured)

Pink

cod roe (pictured)

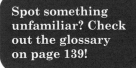

Spot something unfamiliar? Check out the glossary on page 139!

Ingredients for Happy Faces

This colorful guide includes our most commonly used techniques for creating the basic elements of cute bento faces. Mix and match to make your own characters!

Heads

 rice ball head

 hamburger bun head

 hard-boiled egg head

 omelet head

Eyes

 nori eyes

 cheese & nori eyes

 mini chocolate bead eyes

sesame seed eyes

Noses

 carrot nose

 sesame seed nose

 cheese snout

 deli meat snout

Mouths

 nori mouth

 cheese & carrot mouth

 imitation crab mouth

 potato mouth

Hats

 tomato hat

 food pick hat

 cheese hat

mushroom cap

Ears

 fish cake ears

 sausage ears

 cheese horns

sweet potato ears

Hair

 spaghetti hair

 hard-boiled egg hair

 nori hair

 cheese hair

Details

nori hearts

deli meat mittens

imitation crab scarf

cheese buttons

Rice Balls (*Onigiri*)

Compact, portable, and tidy, rice balls are easy to shape into cute heads and bodies.

Deli Meat

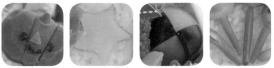

Thinner cuts are easier to wrap around rice or vegetables; thicker slices can be cut into shapes with a knife or cutter.

Veggies

There are myriad ways to use corn, okra, peas, cherry tomatoes, and other veggies to add details and to fill in gaps.

Hot Dogs

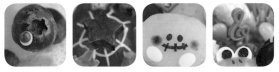

Slice hot dogs in half diagonally for a pretty finish. Or shape them into octopuses, crabs, or flowers. Picks make them easy finger food.

Condiments & Garnishes

Condiments are convenient for adhering noses, eyes, and other features. Food picks and uncooked spaghetti noodles also make great pins.

Nori

Thin, nutritious sheets of nori are made from dried seaweed. They're easy to cut with scissors or punches.

Cheese

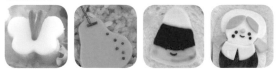

Deli cheese can be cut into endless fun shapes with just a toothpick and your imagination.

Eggs

Peeled hard-boiled eggs can be cut into shapes, decorated, or dyed with food coloring. While still hot, they can be molded into shapes.

Sesame Seeds

Tiny white or black sesame seeds make perfect little eyelashes, flower seeds, and more.

Springtime Fun

Spring is a time of rebirth. The snow melts, flowers begin to bloom, and baby animals come out to play. So let's go outside and enjoy the warm air! Pack a bento box to take along and fill it with in-season veggies like carrots, peas, and potatoes.

Spring Chicken Burger

If you can't find white bread buns, use a regular brown bun instead.

This cheery little burger, a tribute to our egg-laying friends, could not be happier to "spring" into nice weather.

Spring Chicken Burger

- 3 or 4 lettuce leaves
- 1 white bread bun
- 1 Chicken Burger ›
- heart-shaped food pick
- 1 piece nori
- a little mayonnaise
- 1 uncooked spaghetti noodle
- 2 kernels frozen corn
- 1 slice ham or salami
- bento fillers such as tomatoes or fried potatoes

1. Line a bento box with 2 or 3 lettuce leaves.

2. Lightly toast bun. Place burger patty and lettuce on bun. Secure with heart-shaped pick as the chicken's comb.

3. Use a nori punch or scissors to cut out 2 circles of nori. Using a toothpick, apply mayonnaise to the bun. Stick nori circles onto bun as eyes.

4. Break off 4 small pieces of spaghetti noodle. Insert 2 of them into the backs of the corn kernels. Pin corn onto the bun to form a beak.

5. Use a drinking straw to punch 2 circles out of ham or salami. Pierce the circles with the remaining 2 pieces of spaghetti and pin them to the bun as rosy cheeks.

6. Arrange burger in bento box and tuck bento fillers into remaining space.

Chicken Burgers with Sake Sauce
Makes 4 patties

- 3 oz firm tofu
- 5 oz ground chicken
- ½ cup minced onion
- ½ egg, beaten
- 2 tbsp bread crumbs
- 1 tbsp cornstarch
- 1 tsp grated fresh ginger
- several pinches of salt
- a few tsp cooking oil
- ½ cup sake or cooking wine
- 2 tbsp soy sauce
- 4 tsp granulated sugar
- 2 tsp cornstarch

1. Wrap tofu in a double layer of paper towels and place on a dish towel. Place a small pan on top to weigh it down. Let tofu drain for about 20 minutes.

2. In a medium bowl, combine tofu, chicken, onion, egg, bread crumbs, cornstarch, ginger, and salt. Mix well with your hands. Shape mixture into 4 patties.

3. In a large sauté pan, heat a little cooking oil over medium high heat. Add patties and cook for about 5 minutes per side.

4. In a cup, combine sake, soy sauce, sugar, and cornstarch and mix well. Pour into the pan with the patties and cook until sauce thickens. Drain burgers slightly before placing on buns to avoid sogginess.

Butterfly Garden

All you need for colorful butterflies is a flower cutter!

Did you know that butterflies can't fly when the weather is too cold? Fortunately, once winter has passed, they bring a colorful bit of cheer to the once-dreary landscape. They'll add the same charm and grace to your bento.

Butterfly Garden

- enough cooked rice or quinoa to fill half a bento box
- 1 or 2 lettuce leaves
- 1 serving Lemon Salted Fried Chicken (see page 133)
- bento fillers such as thinly sliced sweet potato, okra, or carrot slices
- 1 slice white American cheese
- 1 slice boiled or steamed sweet potato
- 2 pieces boiled okra or 2 sugar snap peas
- 2 slices boiled yellow carrot

1. Fill half of a bento box with rice. Line the other half with lettuce. Arrange Lemon Salted Fried Chicken and bento fillers on top of lettuce.

2. Cut flowers from carrot slices. Optional: make them fancy, as shown below!

3. Stack cheese on sweet potato. With a flower cutter, punch out 2 stacks of flowers.

4. Use a spoon or circle cutter to remove one petal from each stack to create butterflies.

5. With a sharp knife, cut tips off okra pods. Arrange as the butterflies' antennae.

6. Top rice with butterflies and flowers. Tuck remaining okra and carrot pieces into box.

How to Make Vegetable Flowers

❶ Using a flower cutter, punch a flower out of a slice of cooked vegetable such as carrot or potato. With a sharp knife, carefully cut partway into the space between the petals, not pressing all the way through to the bottom.

❷ Tilt the blade and, beginning at the center end of the cut, gently cut at an angle until you reach the edge. Remove the scrap of vegetable.

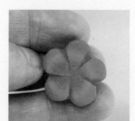

❸ Repeat between all the remaining sets of petals. Garnish with sesame seeds (optional).

Easter Chicks

Baby chicks are one of the first things we all associate with spring. Surround these little ones with fresh seasonal produce and beautiful potato flowers.

Easter Chicks

- enough cooked rice to fill half a bento box
- 1 or 2 lettuce leaves
- 2 thick slices ham
- ½ tsp butter
- a few drops of soy sauce
- ground black pepper to taste
- 3 to 4 tbsp mashed potatoes
- sprig fresh parsley
- 3 Tiny Chicks ⟩
- cherry to garnish (optional)
- pineapple chunks to garnish (optional)

1. Fill half of a bento box with rice, using a fork to pat the top flat. Line the other half with lettuce. Cut ham into bite-sized pieces.

2. In a sauté pan over medium heat, melt butter. Add ham and cook for 1 to 2 minutes, until slightly browned. Sprinkle with soy sauce and pepper. Place ham on lettuce.

3. Fit a pastry bag with a tip and fill with mashed potatoes. Pipe potatoes onto lettuce. Garnish with parsley.

4. Place chicks on rice. Garnish with pineapple chunks and a cherry (if using).

Tiny Chick

- 1 chicken or quail egg, hard-boiled and peeled
- food coloring
- 1 thin slice baby carrot
- 1 piece nori

1. In a small cup or bowl, cover egg with water and add a few drops of food coloring. Let sit until egg is the color you want.

2. Drain egg and discard water.

3. Pinch a small straw into an oval. Use it to cut a beak out of carrot.

4. With a nori punch or scissors, cut eyes and legs out of nori. Apply them to the egg.

> These chicks would be darling on an Easter brunch table!

Easter Nest

For extra flavor, soak the noodles in soba sauce (⅛ cup memmi sauce combined with ½ cup water) before making nests.

Children around the world look forward to Easter's brightly colored eggs and spring animals. You can share in the excitement with this colorful nest of eggs and bunnies. Serve it with fresh, in-season fruit.

Easter Nest

- 1 serving buckwheat soba noodles, cooked according to package directions
- food coloring
- 3 to 5 quail eggs, boiled and peeled
- 1 or 2 purple kale or lettuce leaves
- 1 serving Crab and Daikon Salad ›
- bento fillers such as steamed broccoli, okra, watermelon, or mandarin oranges
- thin slices of ham or fish sausage
- 1 piece nori

1. Wrap a small handful of noodles around four fingers of one hand. Continue wrapping remaining noodles to form a nest. Gently transfer nest to a small bowl. Cover and chill until set.

2. Add a couple drops of food coloring to cups of water, one cup for each color you are using. Soak eggs in water until desired color is achieved. Drain eggs and let dry.

3. Place kale in a bento box. Arrange soba nest on top, tucking in edges with a toothpick as needed. Place Crab and Daikon Salad in a small food cup and add to bento box.

4. Tuck bento fillers into remaining spaces.

5. Using mini shape cutters, cut ham accents for the eggs. Use nori for additional accents or faces for animal shapes. Place eggs in nest.

Crab and Daikon Salad
Makes 2 to 3 servings

- ⅓ cup peeled, julienned daikon or cucumber
- salt to taste
- 1 stick imitation crab (*kanikama*), chopped
- 1 tbsp mayonnaise
- ground black pepper to taste
- pinch of black sesame seeds

1. Lightly sprinkle daikon with salt and let sit for 10 minutes. Pat dry with a clean kitchen towel.

2. In a bowl, combine daikon with imitation crab.

3. Stir in mayonnaise. Season with salt and pepper. Sprinkle with black sesame seeds.

❀ Check the eggs every so often until they reach the desired colors.

Tulip Trio

Who can resist the colors of spring when they come in the form of these smiling tulips? Brightly hued boiled quail eggs bring springtime cheer to your lunch.

Tulip Trio

- food coloring
- 2 quail eggs, hard-boiled and peeled
- enough cooked rice to fill half a bento box, dyed yellow with curry powder (see page 16)
- 1 serving Japanese Curry ›
- bento fillers such as fruits, vegetables, and/or pickles
- small piece nori
- dab of ketchup
- 2 string beans, steamed or boiled

1. Add a couple drops of food coloring to a cup of water. Soak eggs in water until they reach your desired color. Remove from liquid and let dry.

2. Fill half of a bento box with rice, using a fork to pat the top flat. Add Japanese Curry to the other half and tuck in bento fillers.

3. Cut eggs in half. Cut top edges to create the tulip tops. Punch out nori faces and add them to tulips. Use the flat end of a toothpick to dab ketchup on the faces as blushing cheeks.

4. Cut string beans on a diagonal to create leaves. Use the remaining bean pieces as stems. Arrange tulip trio on top of rice.

Japanese Curry
Makes 3 to 4 servings

- 1 lb ground beef or beef stew meat
- ½ cup chopped onion
- 1 medium potato, peeled and cubed
- 1 medium carrot, peeled and cubed
- ½ cup shelled edamame
- 1 4-oz package Japanese curry roux blocks

1. In a large pot over medium-high heat, brown meat. Add onion and cook until tender.

2. Add 3½ cups water, potato, and carrot. Bring to a boil. Lower heat and add edamame. Cover and simmer for about 30 minutes, until vegetables are cooked through.

3. Add curry roux blocks. Stir until curry has dissolved. Simmer uncovered, stirring occasionally, for about 10 minutes, until curry is incorporated.

> Use an aluminum, metal, enamel, or ceramic bento box if you're putting the Japanese Curry directly inside it. The turmeric will dye a plastic box yellow.

Little Piggies

These little piggies wake up early to forage for the best lunch veggies! Set on a bed of fried rice, they will give you energy and cuteness to make it through the day.

Little Piggies

- pink food coloring
- 2 quail eggs or chicken eggs, hard-boiled and peeled
- 1 or 2 lettuce leaves
- 1 serving Breakfast Fried Rice ›
- bento fillers such as tomatoes, cooked breakfast sausage, or peas
- 2 thin slices kamaboko or frozen ham
- small piece nori

1. Add a few drops of food coloring to a bowl of water. Place eggs in water and soak until they turn pink. Drain eggs and dry with paper towels.

2. Line a bento box with lettuce. Add Breakfast Fried Rice, using a fork to pat the top flat. Tuck bento fillers into remaining space.

3. Using a food cutter or a knife, cut 4 ear shapes out of kamaboko. With a nori punch or scissors, cut 4 nori triangles for the inner ears. With the tip of a knife, make a slice approximately the width of the ears in the top of each egg. Gently pry open the cuts and insert the ears. Place nori inner ears on kamaboko ears.

4. Using a piece of drinking straw, cut 2 pig snouts out of kamaboko. With a nori punch, cut out 4 nori eyes and 4 nori nostrils. Place nostrils on pig snouts. Place eyes and noses on the piggies' faces (if they don't adhere, use a slightly moistened toothpick to help). Arrange piggies on top of rice.

Breakfast Fried Rice
Makes 1 serving

- ½ tsp cooking oil
- about ¼ cup chopped ham, sausage, or other meat
- about 1 cup cooked rice
- salt to taste
- ground black pepper to taste
- 1 egg, beaten
- handful fresh or frozen peas
- soy sauce to taste (optional)

1. In a skillet or wok, heat oil over medium-high heat. Add meat and cook, stirring constantly, until slightly browned.

2. Add rice, stirring until well-coated with oil and evenly mixed with meat. Season with salt and pepper. Add egg. Stir until egg is cooked.

3. Add peas and cook, stirring, until peas are bright green. Season with a bit of soy sauce (if using) and toss well.

> Fried rice is best when made with leftover rice. And it's a great way to use other leftovers—just add whatever meats or vegetables you have on hand!

Daffodils spring up so early in the season that they sometimes get snowed on! But they're a sure sign that warmer weather is on its way. Take the opportunity to celebrate with these happy, fresh-faced flowers in a bento.

Dainty Daffodils

- enough cooked rice to fill half a bento box
- 1 or 2 lettuce leaves
- Tsukune ⟩
- thin slices of lemon
- bento fillers such as cooked spinach, grape tomatoes, and pickled vegetables
- 2 slices white American cheese
- 1 slice boiled yellow carrot
- 1 slice yellow American cheese
- 2 boiled edamame
- 2 boiled green beans

1. Fill half of a bento box with rice, using a fork to pat the top flat. Line the other half with lettuce. Arrange Tsukune on lettuce. Garnish with lemon slices and bento fillers.

2. Using a starfish cutter, cut 2 shapes out of the white cheese. Using a flower cutter, cut a flower out of carrot. Arrange on rice.

3. Using a mini flower cutter, cut 1 white cheese flower and 2 yellow cheese flowers. Place them on the centers of the carrot and starfish flowers.

4. With a piece of small drinking straw, cut out 2 white cheese circles and 1 yellow cheese circle. Place them on the mini flowers. Arrange edamame around the flowers as leaves. With a knife, cut more leaves out of green beans and arrange around flowers.

Tsukune (Japanese-Style Chicken Meatballs)
Makes 5 or 6 meatballs

- 9 oz ground chicken
- 1 scallion, finely chopped
- 1 quail egg, beaten, or about 1 tbsp beaten chicken egg
- 1 tbsp cornstarch
- 1 tsp chicken bouillon
- 1 tsp ground ginger
- pinch of salt
- 1 tbsp cooking oil

1. In a large bowl, mix together chicken, scallion, egg, cornstarch, bouillon, ginger, and salt with your hands. Form into 5 or 6 meatballs or small patties.

2. Heat oil in a sauté pan over medium heat. Cook meatballs for 5 to 6 minutes, until browned on both sides and cooked through.

April showers bring May flowers!

Bee in Your Bento

Use a rectangular tamagoyaki pan if you have one.

Buzzy, busy bees make all of spring's beautiful flowers—not to mention harvested food!—possible. Enjoy them in your bento by making them out of tamagoyaki, a Japanese-style rolled omelet.

Bee in Your Bento

- 2 eggs, beaten
- 1 tbsp dashi
- pinch of salt
- pinch of granulated sugar
- a few tsp cooking oil
- enough cooked rice to fill half a bento box
- 1 or 2 lettuce leaves
- Beef and Sweet Potato Rolls (see page 132)
- bento fillers such as tomatoes, boiled spinach sprinkled with bonito flakes, and sweet potato flowers
- 1 piece nori
- 1 slice white American cheese
- red food coloring

1. First, make the tamagoyaki: In a bowl, combine eggs, dashi, salt, and sugar and mix gently. Heat oil in a large pan over medium heat. When hot, use a folded paper towel to spread oil around pan. Add enough egg mixture to coat the bottom of the pan.

2. When the bottom of the egg has started to set but the top is still soft, use a pair of chopsticks to roll over about an inch of egg; continue rolling until you reach the other edge of the pan.

3. Add more egg mixture to the pan, gently lifting the egg roll slightly to allow some uncooked egg underneath. When the bottom has started to set but the top is still soft, roll the egg roll back across the pan, gathering the omelet as you go. Repeat cooking and rolling until egg

mixture is used up and you have a rolled omelet. Let tamogoyaki cool for a few minutes.

4. Using a bamboo mat or plastic wrap, gently shape tamagoyaki into an oval or rectangular tube. Once cooled, cut two 1-inch slices for your honeybee bodies.

5. Fill half of the bento box with rice, using a fork to pat the top flat. Line the other half with lettuce. Tuck Beef and Sweet Potato Rolls and bento fillers into lettuce.

6. Place tamagoyaki slices on top of rice. Using scissors, cut strips of nori and arrange on the bees as stripes. Use a punch to create nori eyes and mouths. Attach them with a slightly moistened toothpick.

7. Use a short piece of thin straw to punch out tiny white American cheese noses. Using a toothpick, dab a tiny bit of red food coloring onto the cheese. Place on bees.

8. Use a heart cutter to create 2 sets of wings from white American cheese. Add to bees.

❖ Gently shape the omelet into a cylinder by wrapping the cooked tamagoyaki in plastic wrap, molding it with your hands, and letting it cool briefly before slicing.

Walking Doggies

These lucky doggies are ready to go!

Springtime isn't fun just for us—our furry friends love it as well! After a long winter inside, they are ready for sunshine, walks, and puddle splashing too. These little pups are happy to go out, rain or shine.

Walking Doggies

- 1 or 2 lettuce leaves
- 2 rice balls (see page 132)
- 2 slices fish cake or 2 slices boiled or steamed potato
- pat of butter
- 1 piece nori
- ¼ slice white American cheese
- 1 cocktail sausage
- 1 serving Chicken and Veggie Stir-Fry >
- bento fillers such as broccoli, peas, or sliced boiled eggs

1. Line a bento box with lettuce. Place rice balls on lettuce.

2. Cut 2 ovals out of fish cake slices. Warm butter in a small pan over low heat. Sauté fish cake slices until lightly browned in the middle. Place on top of rice balls.

3. Cut 2 nori strips and place over the doggies as leashes, using a toothpick to tuck in ends. Use a nori punch to create nori eyes, noses, and paw prints. Apply eyes and paw prints using a slightly moistened toothpick.

4. Pinch a small piece of thick straw into an oval and punch ovals out of cheese as paws. Cut off the tops of the ovals. Apply paws to leashes. Cut small circles for the doggies' noses, applying a small nori dot to each for the tip.

5. Thinly slice sausage and cut edges off for ears. Tuck ears under doggies' heads. Arrange Chicken and Veggie Stir-Fry around rice balls. Accent with bento fillers.

Chicken and Veggie Stir-Fry
Makes 4 to 5 servings

- 7 oz boneless, skinless chicken thighs
- ½ long eggplant
- 1 tbsp oyster sauce
- 1 tbsp sake or cooking wine
- 1 tsp cooking oil
- ½ tsp chopped fresh ginger
- ½ yellow bell pepper, julienned
- salt to taste
- ground black pepper to taste

1. Cut chicken and eggplant into bite-sized pieces. In a small bowl, combine oyster sauce and sake. Set aside.

2. In a sauté pan, heat oil over medium heat. Add chicken and ginger and cook, stirring constantly, until lightly browned. Remove from pan and drain well on paper towels.

3. Wipe the pan clean with a paper towel, return to heat, and stir-fry eggplant and pepper until soft.

4. Add chicken and sauce mixture to the pan. Season with salt and pepper. Cook, stirring and tossing, for 1 minute.

Green Pea Brothers

**Makes
1 bento**

Soon you'll be enjoying fresh spring vegetables such as sweet peas once again. These three pea brothers are tinted green and have tiny pea hands.

Green Pea Brothers

- 1 packet green decofuri or natural food coloring (see page 16)
- 1 cup cooked white rice, still hot
- 1 or 2 lettuce leaves
- 1 slice boiled carrot
- 1 piece nori
- 1 serving Sukiyaki Beef and Quail Egg >
- 6 green peas
- bento fillers such as broccoli or other colorful fruits and vegetables

1. Empty decofuri packet onto hot rice and mix well to incorporate the color, or see Natural Ways to Color Rice on page 16. Form rice into 3 round balls (see page 132).

2. Line a bento box with lettuce. Place rice balls on top, arranging more lettuce between them.

3. Use a drinking straw to cut out 3 carrot noses. Using a nori punch or kitchen scissors, cut out nori eyes and mouths. Place facial features on rice balls.

4. Add Sukiyaki Beef and Quail Egg, cutting egg in half. Add peas as hands. Tuck bento fillers into remaining space.

Sukiyaki Beef and Quail Egg
Makes 2 to 3 servings

- 1 tsp cooking oil
- ¼ lb beef, cut into thin strips
- 1 cup sliced onions
- ½ cup bite-size or sliced mushrooms
- ⅓ cup sake or cooking wine
- 2 tbsp soy sauce
- 1½ tbsp sugar
- 2 or 3 quail eggs, boiled and peeled

1. Heat oil in a sauté pan over medium heat. Add beef and sauté for 1 minute. Add onions and mushrooms and cook for about 1 to 2 minutes, until softened.

2. In a small bowl, combine ½ cup water, sake, soy sauce, and sugar and mix well. Pour into the pan and stir gently.

3. Add eggs and simmer on low heat until liquid has evaporated.

See the glossary on page 139 for more about decofuri and other terms!

Hungry Hippos

A trip to the zoo is the perfect chance to get outside and enjoy warmer weather—and of course pack a bento box. You might even get to see a hippopotamus! Roll up these playful sandwiches to satisfy the hungry hippo in you.

Hungry Hippos

- 1 or 2 slices white bread
- softened butter or mayonnaise
- 2 or 3 slices ham
- 1 or 2 lettuce leaves
- 1 or 2 hot dogs, boiled or pan-fried, or rolled-up cold cuts
- 1 serving Poached Pork Salad ›
- bento fillers such as orange quarters or apple slices
- 2 or 3 slices fish sausage, or more ham
- ¼ slice white American cheese
- 1 piece nori

1. Using a rolling pin, roll bread to flatten. Spread butter on one side of each piece.

2. Cover a cutting board with plastic wrap. Place ham slice on plastic and stack bread on top. Stack 1 lettuce leaf on bread. Place hot dog on one side of the stack. Carefully roll stack around hot dog. Wrap sandwich in plastic. Let set for 5 minutes. Repeat if making 2 sandwiches.

3. With a sharp knife, cut roll(s) into pieces about 1 to 1½ inches long. Line a bento box with lettuce and arrange sandwich pieces on top. Add Poached Pork Salad and bento fillers as needed.

4. Use a small heart cutter to cut 2 hearts out of fish sausage. Cut off the bottom half of each heart to create hippo snouts. Using a piece of drinking straw, cut 4 dots out of fish sausage and place them on the noses. Add snouts to sandwiches.

5. Using a piece of a large drinking straw, cut out 4 eyes from white American cheese. Using a nori punch, cut out nori pupils and place on cheese eyes. Arrange on sandwiches. Use a small knife to cut 4 square teeth out of cheese. Add to the bottom of snouts.

6. Twirl small pieces of ham into hippo ears and tuck into the sides.

Poached Pork Salad
Makes 1 serving

- 2 very thin slices pork
- chopped lettuce
- a few grape tomatoes, halved
- boiled vegetables such as Romanesco broccoli or snap peas
- ¼ slice white bread
- your favorite salad dressing

1. Cut pork into bite-size pieces. Bring a pot of water to a boil over high heat; while it heats, prepare a bowl of ice water. Drop pork into boiling water and cook for 10 seconds, or until cooked through. With chopsticks or tongs, transfer to ice water to cool. Pat dry with paper towel.

2. In a bowl, combine lettuce, tomato, boiled vegetables, and pork.

3. Toast bread. Use a fish cutter to cut several fish out of toast and add to salad.

4. Pack salad dressing separately.

Baby Bird's Nest

As the sun comes out to play, so do the birds. No doubt mama bird is nearby to guard these nests of somen noodles atop a fresh green salad accented with tomato flowers.

Baby Bird's Nest

- 1 serving cooked somen noodles
- salad greens
- 2 to 4 quail eggs, boiled, peeled, and chilled
- black sesame seeds
- 1 baby carrot, steamed or boiled and sliced
- 1 small slice cooked ham
- 2 or 3 cherry or grape tomatoes
- 2 or 3 thin lemon slices

1. Lightly moisten noodles with water so they are easy to handle. Wrap a small bunch of noodles around four fingers of one hand. Continue wrapping noodles until you've used half of the noodles. Place nest into a small bowl. Repeat with remaining noodles and refrigerate for about 1 hour, until set.

2. Fill a bento box with salad greens. Place nests on greens, leaving some leaves sticking up along the sides of the box.

3. Using a knife, carefully cut into the egg white (just barely piercing through to the yolk) and carve a jagged "cracked egg" line around it. Remove the egg white top, leaving the yolk intact. Decorate yolk with black sesame seeds for eyes. Cut a triangle out of carrot and attach as a beak. Repeat with remaining eggs.

4. Using flower cutters, cut out ham and carrot flowers and arrange as garnishes. Sprinkle nests with black sesame seeds.

5. Gently cut the skin from a grape or cherry tomato, starting at the bottom and working your way up the tomato to create a thin spiral strip. Roll and curl the skin—tightly at first and then loosely on the outside—to create a rose. Place roses on lemon slices and place in bento box.

❀ Got leftovers? Extra pieces of vegetables, ham, sausage, and even nori can be used to make a delicious breakfast omelet!

These baby birds would make wonderful additions to a baby shower lunch!

Ladybug Love

These ladybugs have special heart spots for added cuteness!

Who doesn't love teeny ladybugs when they're crawling on a little plant or even up your arm? They're adorable, they eat pesky bugs, and they're a sure sign of spring.

Ladybug Love

* 1 or 2 quail eggs, hard-boiled but still warm
* red or pink food coloring, or shredded beets
* enough cooked rice to fill half a bento box
* lettuce or purple kale
* 1 or 2 Tuna Patties (see page 133), cooled and sliced in half
* bento fillers such as broccoli or boiled sweet potato cut into hearts
* 1 slice ham, rolled into a ham flower
* small piece nori
* 1 piece angel hair pasta, fried

1. Peel eggs before they cool completely. While they are still warm, use your fingers to mold them into perfect circles and gently flatten them. Add a couple drops of food coloring to a cup of water and soak eggs until they reach your desired color. Remove from water and let dry. Carefully slice in half, if desired.

2. Fill half of a bento box with rice, using a fork to pat the top flat. Line the other half with lettuce.

3. Place Tuna Patties on top of lettuce. Tuck in bento fillers and a ham flower (see below).

4. Fold a small strip of nori in half. Using scissors, cut little half hearts on the fold. Open the hearts to use as ladybug spots.

5. Cut out a nori semicircle. Lightly moisten the egg and cover the head of the ladybug with the nori.

6. Add a thin strip of nori to the middle of the ladybug's back. Apply the tiny nori hearts from step 4.

7. Place ladybug on rice. Break off tiny pieces of pasta and attach as antennae.

How to Make a Ham Flower

❶ Fold a round slice of ham in half.

❷ With a sharp knife, make a series of slices along the folded side.

❸ Roll ham and gently separate sliced ends to form petals. Tuck into bento box or secure with toothpick.

Summertime Splash

When summer rolls around, the only logical thing to do is grab your swimsuit and a bento box and head to the pool or the beach for some cool, wet fun. Fortunately, the season offers lots of delicious options to pack, from blueberries and strawberries to fresh carrots and greens. Take advantage of the colorful fruits and veggies in your garden or at the farmers market to pay tribute to the hottest time of the year.

Bouncing Bunnies

Makes
1 bento

Use a heart cutter to make bunny ears—just cut a heart in half down the center!

Bunnies are a favorite of children everywhere for their ears, the way they nibble yummy veggies, and their all-around cuteness. Make sure to watch for them this summer, and in the meantime add these bouncing bunnies to your bento!

Bouncing Bunnies

- 1 or 2 lettuce leaves
- 2 rice balls (see page 132)
- 1 slice fish sausage, kamaboko (fish cake), or boiled sweet potato
- 1 uncooked spaghetti noodle
- 1 piece nori
- Pork Shiso Rolls, sliced >
- bento fillers such as carrot matchsticks, celery matchsticks, or grape tomatoes

1. Line a bento box with lettuce. Top with rice balls.

2. Using a bunny cutter or heart cutter, cut out ears from fish sausage. Use a piece of thick straw to punch out fish sausage arms and legs. Pierce ears, arms, and legs with small pieces of spaghetti and pin them to rice balls.

3. Use scissors or a nori punch to create nori eyes, noses, and mouths. Apply them to rice balls with a slightly moistened toothpick.

4. Arrange Pork Shiso Rolls in the bento box. Tuck in bento fillers.

✿ Pinch a wide straw into an oval shape to cut out arms and legs.

Pork Shiso Rolls
Makes 3 rolls

- ½ carrot
- 6 fresh green beans
- 3 thinly sliced boneless pork chops
- pinch of salt
- pinch of ground black pepper
- 3 to 5 large shiso leaves
- 3 thin slices cooked ham
- 1 tsp cooking oil
- 1 tbsp soy sauce

1. Cut carrot into 6 sticks. Bring a small pot of water to a rolling boil. Add carrots, return to a boil, and cook for 3 minutes. Add green beans and cook for 1 more minute. Carrots should be cooked but firm. Green beans should be bright green. Drain and set aside to cool.

2. Lightly season pork with salt and pepper. Slice green beans in half and place 2 to 3 halves and 2 carrot sticks on one end of the meat. Roll up tightly. Tightly wrap roll in shiso leaf, then ham slice. Secure with a toothpick.

3. In a small sauté pan, heat oil over medium-high heat. Add rolls and cook for 1 to 2 minutes per side, turning with tongs. Drizzle rolls with soy sauce and turn to coat until browned. Transfer to a cutting board to cool.

4. Remove toothpicks. Cut ends off rolls and slice into equally sized pieces.

Ocean Frolic

> If you don't have a starfish cutter, use a regular star cutter and round off the points to create your own starfish.

There's a whole world underneath the ocean, and when it's hot enough outside, we can't help wishing we could explore it, too! This cheerful ocean girl has pretty starfish dancing in her hair and a bright clownfish swimming around with her.

Ocean Frolic

- 2 slices steamed or boiled potato
- 1 to 2 tsp cooking oil
- pinch of salt
- ¼ tsp chopped garlic
- 1 oz spaghetti noodles, cooked al dente and cooled
- ½ tsp soy sauce
- pinch of ground black pepper
- 1 rice ball
- 1 piece nori
- 2 slices boiled carrot
- ¼ slice white American cheese
- 1 or 2 lettuce leaves
- 1 serving Beef and Kimchi Stir-Fry (see page 133)
- bento fillers such as steamed broccoli, peas, or cherry tomatoes

1. With a mini starfish cutter, cut 2 or 3 shapes out of potato; reserve the rest. In a sauté pan, heat oil over medium heat and sauté starfish until lightly browned. Salt. Set aside.

2. Add more oil to the pan, turn heat to low, and stir in garlic. Cook for about 1 minute, until aromatic. Add spaghetti and toss. Add soy sauce and pepper and toss until blended.

3. Place rice ball in a bento box. Arrange spaghetti around it for hair. Decorate with potato starfish.

4. Use a nori punch or scissors to cut out nori eyes and a mouth. Use a piece of drinking straw to cut carrot circles for the nose and cheeks.

5. With a large oval cutter, cut an oval out of the leftover potato. Cut it in half to create hands. Arrange eyes, nose, cheeks, and hands on the rice ball.

6. Make Carrot Clownfish as shown below. Line the rest of the bento box with lettuce. Top with Beef and Kimchi Stir-Fry, bento fillers, and Carrot Clownfish.

How to Make a Carrot Clownfish

❶ Using a fish cutter, cut out a carrot fish and a white American cheese fish.

❷ Using a circle cutter, cut a strip from the cheese fish.

❸ Cut a piece of nori slightly wider than the cheese stripe. Place nori on fish and top with cheese.

Seashell Fun

Pack your Crispy Daikon Cakes with a packet of soy sauce for added flavor!

Beachcombing is a wonderful part of any seaside vacation. Sometimes the intricate shape and texture of an unexpected shell can brighten the whole day. Use mini cutters to create these shell shapes for a noontime meal.

Seashell Fun

- 1 or 2 lettuce leaves
- 2 rice balls (see page 132)
- 2 Crispy Daikon Cakes ›
- ½ boiled cocktail wiener
- bento fillers such as grape tomatoes or sugar snap peas
- 1 slice boiled carrot
- 2 slices raw mountain rose potato
- 2 slices raw potato
- a few peas

1. Line a bento box with lettuce. Place rice balls on lettuce, propping them up slightly. Tuck Crispy Daikon Cakes, cocktail wiener, and bento fillers into bento box.

2. With a mini star cutter, cut stars out of carrot. Make potato seashells as shown below. Boil seashells for 5 minutes. Top rice balls with seashells, carrot stars, and peas.

Crispy Daikon Cakes
Makes 3 to 4 servings

- 8 oz daikon, grated and well drained
- 2 slices ham, chopped
- 1½ oz onion, chopped
- 3 tbsp cornstarch
- 3 tbsp all-purpose flour
- 1 tsp white sesame seeds
- oil for frying

1. Combine all ingredients except oil and mix well.

2. Roll mixture into small dumplings with your hands.

3. In a sauté pan, heat oil over medium heat. Add dumplings and cook for 2 to 3 minutes on each side, until golden brown and cooked through.

How to Make Potato Seashells

❶ Use a heart cutter to cut out a mountain rose potato heart. Cut it in half. Scallop the rounded side with a scallop circle cutter.

❷ Use a small knife to score three or four spiral lines in each shell.

❸ Trim 1 side of potato slice with a scalloped circle cutter.

❹ Use a small circle cutter to round out the bottom of the shape. With a knife, score small strips into the surface to look like grooves on a shell.

Sunbathing Kitties

Mwowr!

These kitties sure know how to survive the lazy days of summer. All they need is a window and some sunshine and they're ready to stretch out and snooze all day.

Sunbathing Kitties

- 2 quail eggs, hard-boiled but still warm
- 2 tbsp memmi sauce or soy sauce
- enough cooked rice to fill half a bento box
- 1 or 2 lettuce leaves
- 1 serving Broccoli and Scallop Stir-Fry >
- bento fillers such as pickled purple cabbage or tomatoes
- 1 slice ham or fish sausage
- 1 piece nori
- dab of ketchup
- peas and carrot stars, for garnish

1. Prepare a bowl of ice water. Peel eggs before they cool completely and, while they are still warm, shape them into spheres with your fingers. Add eggs and memmi sauce to ice water and chill for 5 to 10 minutes, until eggs are brown. Drain eggs and let dry.

2. Place rice in half of a bento box, using a fork to pat the top flat. Line the other half with lettuce and fill it with Broccoli and Scallop Stir-Fry and bento fillers.

3. With a sharp knife, cut ears, tails, and feet out of ham. Gently cut slits in the tops of the eggs (as shown, right) and insert ears.

4. Use a nori punch or kitchen shears to cut facial features and whiskers. Apply them to the eggs with a slightly moistened toothpick.

5. Use a toothpick to dab on rosy ketchup cheeks. Place cats on top of rice. Garnish rice with peas and carrot stars.

Broccoli and Scallop Stir-Fry
Makes 2 servings

- ½ tbsp olive oil
- ½ tsp chopped garlic
- 4 bay scallops
- 4 or 5 broccoli florets, boiled or steamed
- 1 tbsp sake
- pinch of salt
- pinch of ground black pepper
- ½ tsp chopped fresh parsley

1. In a sauté pan, heat oil over low heat. Add garlic and stir for about 30 seconds.

2. Add scallops and cook, stirring constantly, until golden brown on all sides.

3. Stir in broccoli, sake, salt, and pepper. Cover pan and remove from heat, letting broccoli and scallops steam until cooked through.

4. Sprinkle with fresh parsley.

✿ Use a knife to slit open the top of an egg. Then use tweezers to insert ears into the slit.

Sunshine Smile

This smiling summer sun and chipper cloud are flying high! Pack them into your lunch in the summer, or even during the winter when you need a bit of sunshine to warm you up.

Sunshine Smile

- enough cooked rice to fill half a bento box
- 1 or 2 lettuce leaves
- 2 or 3 Japanese-Style Tarama Croquettes ›
- bento fillers such as boiled vegetables or grape tomatoes
- 1 egg, hard-boiled and peeled
- 2 thin slices boiled carrot
- ¼ slice white American cheese
- 1 piece nori
- dab of ketchup
- fresh peas for garnish

1. Fill half a bento box with rice, using a fork to pat the top flat. Line the other half with lettuce leaves and arrange Japanese Style Tarama croquettes and bento fillers on top.

2. Cut egg into thick slices. Use a small knife to cut 9 to 10 little triangles out of carrot. Arrange them around the yolk of one egg slice to create sun rays. Place on top of rice. Reserve remaining egg for another use.

3. Cut a cloud out of cheese and place next to sun. Use a nori punch or scissors to make eyes and mouths for the sun and cloud. Apply them with a slightly moistened toothpick. Dab on ketchup for cheeks.

4. Garnish with peas.

Japanese-Style Tarama Croquettes
Makes 3 to 4 servings (7 or 8 croquettes)

- 10 oz (about 1 cup) mashed potatoes
- 1½ oz cod roe, membrane removed
- 2 tbsp mayonnaise
- 3 tbsp flour
- 1 egg, beaten
- 3 tbsp panko
- oil for frying

1. In a bowl, gently mix mashed potatoes, cod roe, and mayonnaise. Roll into 7 or 8 dumplings with your hands.

2. Dredge dumplings in flour, dip in beaten egg, and roll in panko.

3. Place a wire rack over paper towels; set aside. In a wok or deep skillet over medium heat, warm enough oil to cover dumplings. Place dumplings in hot oil and fry for about 1 to 2 minutes, until golden brown. With tongs, transfer to wire rack to drain and cool.

Flip-Flopping Fun

When you're vacationing at the beach, put on your flip-flops and take a nice, peaceful walk on the sand. This bento will be a sweet reminder of the salty breeze rolling off the ocean.

Flip-Flopping Fun

- enough cooked brown rice to fill half a bento box
- 1 or 2 lettuce leaves
- 1 serving Miso Pork ›
- 1 serving Garlic Green Beans (see page 134)
- bento fillers such as boiled broccoli or tomatoes
- 2 slices boiled sweet potato
- 1 slice boiled carrot
- ¼ slice white American cheese

1. Fill half of a bento box with rice, using a fork to pat the top flat. Line the other half with lettuce. Arrange Miso Pork and Garlic Green Beans on lettuce. Tuck bento fillers into remaining spaces.

2. Use a small knife to cut sweet potato slices into 2 flip-flops. Use a sharp knife to cut 4 thin strips of carrot and place on flip-flops as straps. Arrange flip-flops on rice.

3. Using a mini flower cutter or a knife, cut flowers out of white American cheese. Use a straw to punch circles out of leftover sweet potato and place in the center of white American cheese. Arrange flowers on rice.

Miso Pork
Makes 2 servings

- 2 tbsp miso
- 2 tbsp soy sauce
- 1 tbsp granulated sugar
- ½ tsp grated fresh ginger
- ½ tsp minced garlic
- 1 boneless pork chop
- 1 tsp cooking oil

1. Combine miso, soy sauce, sugar, ginger, and garlic in a plastic zip-top bag. Add pork chop. Squeeze out air and seal bag. Marinate in the refrigerator overnight.

2. Heat oil in a sauté pan over medium high heat. Remove pork chop from the bag and scrape off marinade. Place in oil and cook, flipping once, until browned on both sides, watching carefully so it doesn't burn.

3. Transfer to a cutting board to cool. Cut into bite-size pieces.

This is a lunch you'll flip for!

Turtle and Sailboat

Summer is the time to have fun outside, so treat your family to these sweet little cupcakes featuring fruit turtles instead of frosting. They're irresistible snacks to pack for your own day on the water!

Turtle and Sailboat

- 1 white chocolate pen
- a few chocolate chips
- 1 grape
- 2 blueberries
- 2 mini chocolate beads
- 1 cupcake

1. Place white chocolate pen in hot water to soften. Place chocolate chips in a small bowl and microwave for 10 seconds at a time, stirring between rounds, until melted.

2. With a sharp knife, cut off the bottom third of the grape.

3. Dip a blueberry into melted chocolate and attach it to the grape as the turtle's head.

4. Cut a blueberry into quarters to create the turtle's fins. Use white chocolate pen to draw eyes on the blueberry head. Top with mini chocolate beads as pupils.

5. Place turtle on cupcake and arrange fins around it.

Fruit Sailboats
Makes 2 boats

- 1 strawberry
- 1 grape

1. With a sharp knife, cut strawberry in half, and then trim each half to look like a sail. Cut grape in half.

2. Arrange grape halves cut side up, as the boat bottoms. Use toothpicks to secure the strawberry sails, trimming the toothpicks with kitchen scissors as necessary.

✿ Gently attach the blueberry head to the grape body using melted chocolate as glue.

Make sure fruit is completely dry before it touches melted chocolate, or the chocolate could seize.

Rainbow Sushi

Have you noticed seasoned rice vinegar for sale in your supermarket? That's different from the plain rice vinegar called for here, which you'll season yourself!

Sushi is a balanced, compact way to enjoy a quick meal, making it perfect for packing into a bento box. These rainbow sushi rolls are a colorful new spin on the classic.

Rainbow Sushi

- 1 tbsp Sushi Vinegar >
- 1 cup freshly cooked rice, still hot
- food coloring, store-bought or natural (see page 16)
- ½ cup rice vinegar
- 2 nori sheets
- 1 lettuce leaf
- 1 oz sliced raw sushi-grade salmon
- 1 oz sliced raw sushi-grade tuna
- 2 slices boiled carrot
- 2 or 3 slices avocado
- 1 slice white American cheese
- dab of ketchup

1. In a large bowl, pour Sushi Vinegar over hot rice. Mix gently until cooled. Separate rice into equal portions. Dye each a different color.

2. Roll and slice sushi as shown below, using rice, 1 nori sheet, lettuce, salmon, tuna, carrot, and avocado. Arrange sushi slices on a plate, removing the plastic wrap.

3. Use a cloud cutter to cut clouds out of cheese. Use a nori punch to cut out nori eyes and mouths. Place faces on clouds. Use a toothpick to dab on ketchup cheeks.

4. Using mini cutters, cut stars and dots out of remaining avocado and carrot slices. Arrange shapes on sushi.

Sushi Vinegar
Makes enough for 3 cups cooked rice

- 3 tbsp rice vinegar
- 3 tsp salt
- 3 tbsp granulated sugar

In a small bowl, stir together vinegar and salt. Add sugar and stir until dissolved. Refrigerate until ready to use.

How to Roll Sushi

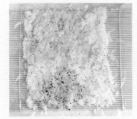

❶ Cover a bamboo mat with plastic wrap. Wet your fingers with vinegar. Spread colored rice on plastic and flatten into a rectangle.

❷ Top rice with nori sheet. Place lettuce, salmon, tuna, carrot, and avocado partway up one side of the nori.

❸ Roll the sushi with the bamboo mat, lifting the end of the plastic wrap as you work to avoid rolling it into the sushi.

❹ Wrap the sushi roll in the plastic wrap. With a knife, cut roll into pieces. Wipe the knife between each cut to prevent sticking.

The heat of summer is the perfect excuse to eat ice cream. With this bento, you can have all the fun of an ice cream cone with none of the sugar!

We All Scream for Ice Cream

- enough cooked rice to fill half a bento box
- 1 or 2 lettuce leaves
- 3 or 4 pieces Garlic Chicken (see page 134)
- small cup of Frozen Fruit Salad (see page 136)
- bento fillers such as sweet potato, broccoli, tomatoes, or pickles
- ½ slice white American cheese
- ½ slice yellow American cheese
- ½ slice ham
- 4 black sesame seeds
- 1 piece nori
- dab of ketchup
- 1 or 2 slices sweet potato
- a little cooking oil

1. Fill half of a bento box with rice, using a fork to pat the top flat. Line the other half with lettuce. Arrange Garlic Chicken, Frozen Fruit Salad, and bento fillers on lettuce.

2. Draw a scoop of ice cream on parchment paper and cut it out. Place paper shape on top of white cheese. Using a toothpick, gently cut out 2 shapes from the cheese.

3. Place cheese scoops at the edge of the yellow cheese and cut out cone shapes with a knife or toothpick. Use a slightly moistened toothpick to score the cones with crisscrossed lines. Place ice cream cones on top of ham and cut around them using a knife. Ham will provide contrast against rice.

4. Place 2 sesame seed eyes on each ice cream cone. With scissors or a nori punch, cut out nori noses and mouths and place under eyes. Dab on some ketchup cheeks with the flat end of a toothpick.

5. Arrange ice cream cones on rice.

6. With a knife or star cutter, cut shapes out of sweet potato. Heat oil in a small sauté pan over medium-high heat. Add sweet potato stars and cook, flipping once, until golden brown. Arrange on rice next to ice cream cones.

❀ Keep the side of the parchment that you wrote on face up so that pencil marks don't touch the cheese.

Twirl the toothpick as you cut, and moisten it as needed, so the cheese doesn't tear.

Playing It Cool

When the sun is blazing hot, what's your go-to food for cooling off? These baseball players like watermelon best!

Playing It Cool

- 1 or 2 lettuce leaves
- 2 rice balls (see page 132)
- Vegetable Tempura ❯
- bento fillers such as asparagus slices or shrimp
- 1 stick imitation crab (*kanikama*)
- 1 thin slice cucumber
- 5 or 6 black sesame seeds
- 1 piece nori
- ⅛ slice white American cheese
- 2 hat-shaped food picks
- 1 slice boiled sweet potato

1. Line a bento box with lettuce. Add rice balls. Arrange pieces of Vegetable Tempura around rice balls. Tuck in bento fillers.

2. Peel imitation crab, preserving the red outer "skin." Using a small round metal cutter—ideally one that matches the diameter of the cucumber—cut a circle out of the skin.

3. Stack crab circle on cucumber slice. Cut into wedges. Arrange watermelon slices on rice balls. Place sesame seeds on each watermelon slice. Use a nori punch or kitchen scissors to make 4 nori eyes. Place on rice balls.

4. Use a piece of thick straw to cut out a circle from a leftover piece of crab skin. Cut it in half and place pieces on rice balls as smiles.

5. Use a piece of straw to cut 4 circles from the cheese. Add to watermelon slices as hands. Add hat picks to rice balls. Cut 2 wedges from the sweet potato for hair and place on heads.

Vegetable Tempura
Makes 1 to 2 servings

- ½ cup all-purpose flour
- ¼ cup ice water
- 1 asparagus stalk or green bean
- 2 to 3 zucchini or eggplants, cut into matchsticks
- 1 thinly sliced sweet potato
- cooking oil

1. In a bowl, mix flour and ice water. Dip one of the vegetables in the mixture; it should be thick enough to coat the vegetable. If it slides off, chill mixture in freezer for 10 minutes to thicken.

2. In a wok or deep skillet, warm enough oil to cover the vegetables. Set out a wire rack or line a plate with paper towels.

3. Cut asparagus into bite-size pieces, stack, and secure with a toothpick. Dip vegetables in batter, place in hot oil, and fry for about 2 minutes, until tempura is golden and the bubbles in the oil get smaller. Using tongs, transfer to a wire rack to drain.

> If you have leftover tempura batter, mix it with julienned carrots and onions. Drop small spoonfuls into the oil to make fritters.

Cheerful Crab

This bento is perfect for a day at the beach!

This cheerful crab has been scuttling along on the hot sand, dodging giant beachgoers and tiny rocks. His cute smile is infectious!

Cheerful Crab

- enough cooked rice to fill half a bento box
- 1 or 2 lettuce leaves
- 2 Cream Corn Croquettes (see page 136)
- 1 serving Chicken and Cabbage Salad >
- 2 cherry tomatoes, approximately the same size, 1 red and 1 orange
- bento fillers such as boiled broccoli or corn
- 2 or 3 cocktail wieners
- 1 uncooked spaghetti noodle
- ¼ slice white American cheese
- 1 piece nori

1. Fill half of a bento box with rice, using a fork to pat the top flat. Line the other half with lettuce.

2. Place 1 croquette on lettuce, cutting in half if necessary to fit. Arrange Chicken and Cabbage Salad next to croquette. Place remaining croquette on top of rice.

3. Cut both tomatoes into quarters. Reassemble 4 pieces with alternating colors to look like a beach ball. Tuck beach ball and bento fillers into remaining spaces.

4. Cut 2 crab pincers out of the wieners and arrange them near the croquette. Slice the remaining wieners into legs and attach to the croquette with spaghetti (if needed).

5. Use a piece of thick straw to cut 2 eyes out of cheese. Attach to the top of the croquette with a piece of spaghetti. Cut out nori pupils and place on cheese.

6. Cut a laughing mouth out of cheese and place it on the croquette.

Chicken and Cabbage Salad
Makes 5 to 6 servings

- 3 oz chicken breast, fat and skin removed
- 9 oz cabbage, shredded or sliced
- 2 ½ oz frozen corn kernels, cooked or thawed
- 1 ½ tbsp mayonnaise
- salt to taste
- ground black pepper to taste

1. Over high heat, bring a pot of water to a boil. Add chicken and boil for 3 minutes. Add cabbage to boiling water and cook for 30 seconds. Drain and let cool.

2. With your fingers, pull chicken into bite-size pieces. Firmly press cabbage into a strainer with your hands to drain well.

3. In a bowl, gently mix chicken, cabbage, corn, and mayonnaise to combine. Sprinkle with salt and pepper.

Summer is baseball season, and hot dogs are a favorite whether you're playing or visiting the ballpark. These mini hot dogs will be a homerun in any lunch.

Hot Diggity Dogs

- enough cooked rice to fill half a bento box
- 1 or 2 lettuce leaves
- 1 serving Shrimp Stir-Fry >
- bento fillers such as pickled cucumbers
- 2 cocktail wieners
- ¼ slice American cheese
- ketchup to taste
- fresh peas for garnish

1. Fill half a bento box with rice, using a fork to pat the top flat. Line the other half with lettuce.

2. Arrange Shrimp Stir-Fry on lettuce. Tuck bento fillers into remaining spaces.

3. Cut a V-shaped slice out of each cocktail wiener to create the bun. Heat a small sauté pan over medium heat, add wieners and cut-out slices, and cook until lightly browned. Set aside to cool.

4. Arrange small pieces of lettuce, wiener slices, and strips of cheese in sliced wieners. Set small pieces of parchment paper on rice and place assembled hot dogs on top. Drizzle with ketchup. Garnish with fresh peas.

Shrimp Stir-Fry
Makes 3 to 4 servings

- 10 to 12 small shrimp, peeled and deveined
- oil for frying
- ½ garlic clove, minced
- 1 to 2 tbsp chopped celery
- 4 tbsp sweet chili sauce
- 3 tbsp sake or white wine
- 1 tbsp chopped green onion
- pinch of salt
- pinch of ground black pepper

1. Use paper towels to pat shrimp dry.

2. Heat oil in a skillet over medium heat. Add garlic and cook for about 30 seconds, until fragrant. Add shrimp and celery and cook, stirring constantly, until shrimp turns pink.

3. In a small cup, combine chili sauce and sake. Add to shrimp and cook, stirring constantly, for 1 minute, or until cooked through. Stir in green onion, salt, and pepper.

❁ Cut out strips of parchment paper to give your mini hot dogs a fun ballpark feel.

Play ball!

Singing Frogs

**Makes
1 bento**

Summer nights are anything but quiet—when the weather is warm, frogs come out to sing. What do you think these two colorful frogs are singing about?

Singing Frogs

- enough cooked rice to fill half a bento box
- 1 or 2 red leaf lettuce leaves
- 2 Curry Chicken Nuggets ›
- bento fillers such as broccoli, pickles, or steamed edamame
- 2 cherry tomatoes, 1 green and 1 red
- ¼ slice white American cheese
- 1 piece nori
- 4 black sesame seeds
- 1 piece baby corn
- musical food picks

1. Fill half of a bento box with rice, using a fork to pat the top flat. Line the other half with lettuce. Arrange Curry Chicken Nuggets and bento fillers on lettuce.

2. Using a sharp knife, cut a small wedge from each tomato to create mouths. Cut a slit into the top of each tomato for the eyes. Use a piece of straw to cut eyes out of cheese. Use a nori punch or kitchen scissors to cut nori pupils and apply to eyes. Insert eyes into slits. Add sesame seeds as noses.

3. Place frogs on rice. Add musical food picks.

4. Slice baby corn into rounds and add as garnish.

Curry Chicken Nuggets
Makes 3 to 4 servings

- 8 oz ground chicken
- 3 oz tofu, drained and crumbled
- 5 oz chopped onion (about 1 small onion)
- 2 quail eggs or ½ chicken egg, beaten
- 3 tsp bread crumbs
- 1½ tbsp cornstarch
- ½ tbsp curry powder
- ⅓ tsp garlic powder
- ⅓ tsp salt
- oil for frying
- sweet chili sauce to taste (optional)

1. In a large bowl, combine all ingredients except oil and chili sauce, using your hands to mix well.

2. Roll into 8 to 10 dumplings.

3. In a sauté pan, heat oil over medium heat. Add dumplings and cook, flipping once, until golden brown on each side. Season with sweet chili sauce, if using.

If the sesame seeds don't stick on their own, dab on mayonnaise to help.

Fall Frenzy

After summer, the leaves change color and the weather becomes blustery and cool. Animals and people alike begin to bring in abundant harvests and store them for winter. These bentos celebrate the bounty with busy squirrels, holidays such as Halloween and Thanksgiving, and more.

New School Year Fun

Say hello to a
new school year!

buono

Although it's wonderful to see friends again when school starts, some kids come down with a case of the back-to-school blues. Help them get back into the groove with this friendly bus-themed bento.

New School Year Fun

- 2 quail eggs, hard-boiled but still warm
- enough cooked rice to fill half a bento box
- 1 or 2 lettuce leaves
- Grilled Cod ›
- bento fillers such as broccoli or tomatoes
- 1 slice cheddar cheese
- 1 slice white American cheese
- 1 piece nori
- 1 piece salami
- red food coloring
- 1 slice ham
- 1 slice boiled sweet potato

1. Peel eggs before they cool. While still warm, mold them into spheres with your fingers.

2. Fill half of a bento box with rice, using a fork to pat the top flat. Line the other half with lettuce. Fill with Grilled Cod and bento fillers.

3. Cut cheddar cheese into a rectangle to form the bus. Cut squares out of white American cheese and place them on the bus as windows. Cut 2 strips of nori and place them on the bus to form stripes.

4. Place bus on top of rice. Cut 2 circles out of salami. Place on the bus as wheels. Use a piece of drinking straw to cut a circle of white American cheese. Use a toothpick to paint the cheese red with food coloring. Add to bus.

5. Cut eggs in half and place the rounder bottom halves onto the bus windows. Cut ears and arms out of ham. Use a thin drinking straw to cut snouts out of ham. Place arms, ears, and snouts on the piggies.

6. Using a nori punch or kitchen scissors, cut 4 nori eyes, 2 smiles, and 4 nostrils for the piggies. Arrange them on their faces.

7. Use a knife or food cutter to cut a cloud or sun out of sweet potato. Add to bento box. Garnish with ham and nori to create a happy face.

Grilled Cod
Makes 1 serving

- 3 oz cod fillet, cut into 2 or 3 pieces
- pinch of salt
- pinch of ground black pepper
- 2 slices prosciutto
- ½ tbsp all-purpose flour
- a few tsp cooking oil
- ½ garlic clove, minced
- 3 bite-sized pieces boiled potato
- 4 or 5 rosemary leaves

1. Season cod with salt and pepper. Wrap in prosciutto and sprinkle with flour.

2. In a medium pan, heat oil over low heat and add garlic. Cook for about 1 minute, until tender.

3. Add potato and cod. Cook, stirring carefully, for about 4 minutes, until cod is golden brown. Sprinkle with rosemary.

Chattering Squirrel Pal

If you don't have a bear cutter, trace the squirrel head on parchment paper and cut out the shape. Then place the paper on a carrot and trace around it with a sharp knife.

When autumn comes around, squirrels go into a frenzy storing food for the winter! Here's how to turn a bear shape into a squirrel to make the most of your food cutters.

Chattering Squirrel Pal

- enough cooked rice to fill half a bento box
- 2 or 3 lettuce leaves
- 2 pieces Pork Mushroom Roll (see page 132)
- bento fillers such as steamed vegetables
- 1 thick slice boiled carrot
- ½ slice white American cheese
- 1 piece nori
- 1 piece ham or salami
- 2 Sausage Acorns >

1. Fill half a bento box with rice, using a fork to pat the top flat. Line the other half with lettuce. Add Pork Mushroom Roll and fillers.

2. Make a squirrel head as shown below, using carrot slice and white American cheese.

3. Using a nori punch, cut out 2 nori circles for the eye and nose. Cut out a cheese circle for nose. Stack nori on top of cheese and arrange on face. Place eye on squirrel face. Use a piece of drinking straw to cut rosy cheeks out of ham and add to face.

4. Arrange squirrel head and Sausage Acorns on rice. With a mini flower cutter, cut remaining carrot into flowers for garnish.

Sausage Acorns
Makes 2 acorns

- 1 mini sausage
- ¼ slice white American cheese
- food picks or toothpicks

Cut sausage in half. Cut 2 circles out of cheese to make acorn caps. Stack one on the flat part of each sausage. Secure with food picks.

How to Make a Squirrel Head

❶ Use a mini bear cutter to cut a bear shape out of carrot.

❷ Use a knife to remove 1 ear to form the squirrel's head.

❸ Cut a bear shape out of cheese. Turn the bear cutter upside down and cut out a football-shaped piece for the squirrel's face. Place face on the head.

A Pear Anywhere

MERCI

The perfect lunch
pearing!

Fall is a time of bounty. Apple orchards open for picking, and juicy pears are ready to harvest. Celebrate the fall harvest with this adorable plump pear bento.

A Pear Anywhere

- enough cooked rice to fill half a bento box, dyed a color of your choice (see page 16)
- 1 or 2 lettuce leaves
- 2 or 3 pieces Easy Yakitori Chicken ›
- bento fillers such as boiled broccoli, tamagoyaki (see page 37), or sweet black beans
- 1 slice yellow American cheese
- 1 slice white American cheese
- 1 boiled green bean
- 1 fried spaghetti noodle
- 1 piece nori or black sesame seeds
- a few peas for garnish

1. Fill half of a bento box with dyed rice, using a fork to pat the top flat. Line the other half with lettuce. Add Easy Yakitori Chicken and bento fillers.

2. Stack cheese slices. Use a pear cutter or a toothpick and parchment paper (see page 67) to cut out 2 pear stacks.

3. Place pears on rice. Cut leaves out of green bean and arrange on pears. Add pieces of fried spaghetti noodle as stems.

4. With a nori punch or piece of a small drinking straw, punch out tiny nori circles and apply as spots on pears. Alternatively, press black sesame seeds into pears. Garnish with peas.

Easy Yakitori Chicken
Makes 2 skewers (about 4 to 6 pieces)

- 2 oz boneless, skinless chicken breast
- pinch of salt
- pinch of ground black pepper
- cooking oil
- Basic Teriyaki Sauce (page 136), optional

1. Soak wooden skewers in water for 10 minutes before using to avoid burning them on the grill.

2. Cut chicken into bite-size pieces. Pat dry. Preheat a grill to medium heat.

3. Thread chicken onto skewers. Brush lightly with oil to prevent sticking. Season with salt and pepper.

4. Grill chicken for 4 to 5 minutes, turning occasionally, until golden brown on all sides. Cover with Basic Teriyaki Sauce (if using).

Falling Leaves & Acorns

This tasty lunch pays tribute to the beautiful colors of autumn's foliage. Don't forget to bring your bento box on your next leaf-peeping excursion!

Falling Leaves & Acorns

- enough cooked rice to fill half a bento box
- 1 or 2 lettuce leaves
- 2 or 3 Pan-Fried Scallops >
- bento fillers such as Romanesco broccoli or halved cherry tomatoes
- 1 red cocktail wiener
- 2 boiled shimeji mushroom caps or black olives
- 1 slice boiled sweet potato
- 1 slice boiled carrot
- pinch of black sesame seeds
- 3 or 4 steamed green peas

1. Fill half of a bento box with rice, using a fork to pat the top flat. Line the other half with lettuce and top lettuce with Pan-Fried Scallops. Tuck bento fillers into remaining space.

2. Cut cocktail wiener in half. Use toothpicks to attach mushroom caps to the flat ends to create acorns.

3. Use mini leaf cutters to cut shapes out of sweet potato and carrot.

4. Arrange acorns, leaves, sesame seeds, and green peas on top of rice.

Pan-Fried Scallops
Makes 1 serving

- ¼ cup panko
- 1 tsp minced fresh parsley
- 1 tbsp all-purpose flour
- ½ egg, beaten
- oil for frying
- 2 or 3 small scallops
- pinch of salt
- pinch of ground black pepper

1. In a small bowl, combine panko and parsley. Place flour in another small bowl and beaten egg in a third.

2. Heat oil in a small pan over medium-high heat.

3. Season scallops with salt and pepper. Dust with flour, coating all sides.

4. Dip scallops in egg and dredge in panko mixture. Fry for about 5 minutes, until golden brown and cooked through.

If you make a Chattering Squirrel Pal (see page 80), be sure it doesn't hop over and snatch up your acorns!

Nom-Nom Bear

This cuddly bear is pleased as can be to nosh on a bunch of sweet grapes. He's got lots to load up on because it's almost time to hibernate!

Nom Nom Bear

- enough cooked rice to fill half a bento box
- 1 or 2 lettuce leaves
- 1 Chinese Egg Roll (see page 134)
- bento fillers such as boiled vegetables, tomatoes, or buttered corn
- 2 slices boiled sweet potato
- 1 uncooked spaghetti noodle
- ¼ slice white American cheese
- 1 slice boiled carrot
- 1 piece nori
- 4 green peas
- 1 slice boiled purple sweet potato or purple potato
- 1 boiled broccoli stem

1. Fill half of a bento box with rice, using a fork to pat the top flat. Line the other half with lettuce. Cut Chinese Egg Roll in half and place it on lettuce. Tuck in bento fillers.

2. Use a bear cookie cutter to cut 2 bear heads out of sweet potato. Turn one head shape upside down and attach it to the other bear's chin with pieces of spaghetti to make a body as shown. Place on top of rice. Use a drinking straw to cut a tail out of sweet potato and arrange on bear.

3. Use a piece of drinking straw to cut out 5 cheese circles. Arrange as the bear's nose, hands, and feet.

4. Use a piece of small drinking straw to punch out 4 carrot circles. Arrange as the bear's cheeks and paws.

5. Using a nori punch or scissors, cut out nori eyes, nose, mouth, and footprints. Apply them with a slightly moistened toothpick. Place green pea to cover the spaghetti noodle on the bear's chin.

6. Use a piece of drinking straw to cut out purple potato circles and arrange next to the bear as grapes, adding some peas as green grapes as well. With a mini leaf cutter, cut out a broccoli stem leaf and arrange next to grapes.

Night Owl

Hoo is she looking at?

This owl is curious and inquisitive! Her big, bright eyes let her see the world around her.

Night Owl

- enough cooked rice to fill half a bento box
- 1 or 2 lettuce leaves
- 1 serving Easy Barbecue Chicken >
- sprinkle of Parmesan cheese
- bento fillers such as broccoli, fried zucchini, or tomatoes
- 1 slice ham
- ¼ slice white American cheese
- 1 piece nori
- ⅛ slice yellow American cheese
- 1 slice boiled purple sweet potato or purple potato
- cooking oil
- 2 or 3 green peas

1. Fill half of a bento box with rice, using a fork to pat the top flat. Line the other half with lettuce.

2. Place Easy Barbecue Chicken on top of lettuce. Sprinkle with Parmesan cheese. Tuck in fillers.

3. Stack ham on white American cheese. Use an oval cutter and a mini star food cutter to cut out the owl's head and ears. Arrange pieces on rice.

4. With a piece of thick drinking straw, cut out white cheese eyes. With a smaller straw, cut out pink ham eyes. Place pink eyes on white eyes. With a nori punch, punch out pupils and place them on eyes.

5. With a knife, cut a triangle out of yellow cheese. Place beak on the face. Cut another triangle from white cheese and place on one side as a wing.

6. Use a small pair of scissors to cut out strips of nori for the owl's feathers and place below face.

7. With a large cutter or knife, cut a star out of purple sweet potato. In a small sauté pan over medium heat, warm a little oil. Sauté potato for a few minutes. Arrange on rice. Garnish with green peas.

Easy Barbecue Chicken
Makes 3 to 4 servings

- 10 oz boneless, skinless chicken thighs
- pinch of salt
- pinch of ground black pepper
- 1 tbsp all-purpose flour
- 1 tsp butter
- 5 oz grated onion (about 1 small onion)
- 1 cube chicken bouillon
- 2 tbsp ketchup

1. Cut chicken into bite-size pieces. Pat dry with paper towels. Season with salt and pepper and sprinkle with flour.

2. In a sauté pan over medium heat, melt butter. Add chicken and onion and cook, stirring constantly, until browned.

3. In a small bowl, combine 1 cup of water, bouillon cube, and ketchup. Pour into sauté pan with chicken and onion and simmer over low heat for about 10 minutes, until liquid has almost evaporated.

Fried Rice Jack-o-Lantern

Show your boo colors!

The best part about Halloween is the spooky-but-cute atmosphere that people of all ages enjoy. This jack-o-lantern grins while his two little skeleton buddies snicker above, no doubt up to some mischief.

Fried Rice Jack-o-Lantern

- 1 to 2 tsp olive oil
- 1 cup cooked rice
- 1 tbsp ketchup
- pinch of salt
- pinch of ground black pepper
- 1 slice white American cheese
- 1 piece nori
- 1 green bean
- 1 or 2 lettuce leaves
- 2 Quail Egg Skeletons ›
- bento fillers such as okra, tomatoes, or zucchini

1. In a sauté pan, heat oil over medium-high heat. Add rice and toss lightly. Add ketchup, salt, and pepper. Toss until mixture is well blended and rice is orange.

2. Line a work surface with plastic wrap and place fried rice on the plastic. Use your hands to bundle it up and form it into a jack-o-lantern shape. Carefully unwrap and place rice in a bento box or on a plate.

3. Use a drinking straw to punch out 2 cheese eyes. Use a pair of scissors or a nori punch to create pupils and a mouth. Be creative and make your own face, just as you would on a real pumpkin! Arrange pieces on rice. Insert a piece of green bean into the top of the jack-o-lantern to form the stem.

4. Line the rest of the bento box with lettuce. Add Quail Egg Skeletons and tuck in bento fillers.

Quail Egg Skeletons
Makes 2 skeletons

- 2 quail eggs, hard-boiled but still warm
- 2 1-inch pieces fish cake or sausage
- 1 piece nori

1. Prepare a bowl of ice water. Peel eggs before they cool completely. While still warm, mold them into spheres with your fingers. Chill in ice water to set the shape. Drain.

2. Use toothpicks to attach quail egg heads to fish cake bodies.

3. Use a fork-shaped punch to create nori arms, eyes, and mouths. Apply to skeletons with a slightly moistened toothpick.

❁ If you don't have a fork-shaped punch, use a small pair of scissors or the nori punch of your choice.

Mini Mummies

As Halloween creeps closer, draw sleepy children out of their comfy beds with these adorable breakfast mummies. You can also serve them as snacks at your spooktacular Halloween party—they're easy and fun to make!

Mini Mummies

- cooking spray
- 1 8-oz can crescent roll dough
- 12 cocktail wieners
- 1 piece nori
- 1 slice white American cheese, optional
- dab of ketchup
- lettuce leaves

1. Preheat oven according to the dough package instructions. Spray a baking sheet with cooking spray.

2. Unroll dough and separate into precut triangles. Use a knife to cut each triangle into 8 thin strips, each about ⅓ inch wide.

3. Carefully wrap each cooled sausage with dough strips, pulling the dough gently so that it can enclose the sausage a few times. Make sure to cross the dough strips over each other to form the mummy's bandages.

4. Place wrapped sausages on the prepared baking sheet and bake for 9 to 10 minutes, or until lightly browned. Meanwhile, punch out nori eyes and cheese circles (if using).

5. When mummies are cool, place the nori circles on cheese circles and arrange eyes on mummies. With a toothpick, dab on ketchup cheeks.

6. Serve on lettuce for garnish.

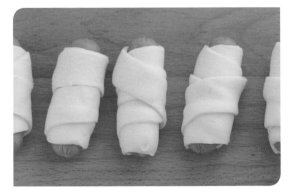

❀ Cross the crescent roll strips over each other for best mummy style.

❀ Arrange orange slices in a pumpkin shape to complete your Halloween breakfast.

Boil the wieners for 1 minute to make them rounder and plumper. Let them cool before wrapping in dough.

Halloween Cuties

Instantly improve a boring sandwich with these Halloween cuties, cut from slices of cheese. They're fun to make with kids and easy to attach to a simple sandwich. You can even serve them on a bagel with cream cheese for breakfast.

Halloween Cuties

- sliced yellow American cheese
- sliced white American cheese
- food coloring
- nori
- sandwiches

1. With a knife or parchment paper and a toothpick (see page 67), cut both cheeses into Halloween shapes, such as Frankenstein, witches, skeletons, ghosts, jack-o-lanterns, devils, and candy corn.

2. Drop dots of food coloring on a sheet of waxed paper. Using a toothpick as your "brush," paint details onto cheese shapes.

3. With a nori punch or scissors, cut out nori faces. Use a slightly moistened toothpick to apply to cheese characters.

4. Top sandwiches with Halloween Cuties.

To spookify your lunch even more, try making purple or green breads in your bread machine using store-bought or natural food coloring. Simply add it to the ingredients before starting the machine.

Lil' Ghosts

Boo! Halloween is one of the most entertaining holidays to make bento for, and these ghosts are ready to bring smiles and giggles with their goofy skeleton-like grins. Anything for a good scare!

Lil' Ghosts

- ❧ enough rice to fill half a bento box
- ❧ 1 or 2 lettuce leaves
- ❧ 1 serving Spicy Minced Pork Salad ›
- ❧ bento fillers such as tomatoes, okra, or pickles
- ❧ 2 slices boiled sweet potato
- ❧ 1 piece nori
- ❧ dab of ketchup
- ❧ ¼ slice white American cheese
- ❧ 1 slice boiled carrot
- ❧ Halloween-themed food picks such as bats, pumpkins, or spooky leaves (optional)

1. Fill half of a bento box with rice, using a fork to pat the top flat. Line the other half with lettuce. Fill lettuce with spoonfuls of Spicy Minced Pork Salad. Tuck in bento fillers.

2. Use a circle cutter to cut 2 shapes out of sweet potato.

3. Use a nori punch and kitchen scissors to make 4 eyes, 2 mouths, and 6 lines for stitches. Use a slightly moistened toothpick to attach pieces to ghosts. Dab on ketchup cheeks with a toothpick. Use a drinking straw to cut 4 hands out of cheese and place onto ghosts. Arrange ghosts on rice.

4. Use a star cutter to cut a star out of carrot. Place on rice. Decorate with food picks (if using).

Spicy Minced Pork Salad

Makes 2 to 3 servings

- ❧ 1 tsp cooking oil
- ❧ ½ garlic clove, minced
- ❧ 7 oz minced or ground pork
- ❧ 2 or 3 fresh basil leaves, chopped
- ❧ 2 tbsp green peas
- ❧ 1 tbsp fish sauce
- ❧ salt to taste
- ❧ ground black pepper to taste

1. In a sauté pan, heat oil over low heat. Add garlic and cook for about 30 seconds, until fragrant.

2. Add pork and basil, stirring until pork is light brown and almost fully cooked.

3. Sprinkle in peas, fish sauce, salt, and pepper.

We're your favorite lunch haunts!

Frowny Frankie

When you make Stir-Fried Okra with Bacon, don't forget to set aside a piece of okra for Frowny Frankie's nose.

Dr. Frankenstein's monster doesn't look very happy, but that fits his character! No doubt the sassy little ghost next to him adds to his frowny funk. Can you resist sticking your tongue back at it?

Frowny Frankie

- 1 cup cooked rice
- 1 package green decofuri or green food coloring
- pinch of salt
- ½ sheet nori
- 1 or 2 lettuce leaves
- 1 tbsp mayonnaise
- 1 okra stem
- ⅛ slice white American cheese
- 1 quail egg, hard-boiled and peeled
- 1 grape tomato
- 1 serving Stir-Fried Okra with Bacon ›
- bento fillers such as shredded carrot
- 2 slices boiled purple sweet potato

1. Divide rice in half. Color one half green, using either green decofuri or a little bit of diluted green food coloring (not too much!). Shape green rice into a ball.

2. Sprinkle salt onto remaining rice. Shape into a ball. Cover ball completely with a piece of nori, moistening the edges with water to seal.

3. Cut Frankie's zigzag hair out of a piece of nori. Wrap half the green rice ball with it.

4. Line a bento box with lettuce. Add rice balls.

5. Spoon mayonnaise onto a piece of plastic wrap, wrap it up, and secure ends with a rubber band. Cut a small slit in plastic and pipe a spiderweb of mayo onto the black rice ball.

6. Use scissors and a nori punch to cut out nori eyes, mouth, eyebrow, and stitches. Apply to Frankie's face with a slightly moistened toothpick. Use okra stem for his nose. Use a mini cutter or small knife to cut hands out of cheese. Arrange under his chin.

7. Cut a small wedge out of quail egg. Cut a tongue out of tomato and insert it into egg. Cut out nori eyes and apply them.

8. Tuck in ghost, Stir-Fried Okra with Bacon, and bento fillers. With a knife or star cutter, cut stars out of purple sweet potato. Arrange them in the bento box.

Stir-Fried Okra with Bacon
Makes 1 serving

- 1 slice bacon
- 2 okra stalks, chopped
- 2 or 3 grape or cherry tomatoes, halved
- pinch of salt
- pinch of ground black pepper

1. Heat a skillet over medium heat. Add bacon and fry until crispy. Transfer bacon to a wire rack to drain, reserving some grease in the pan. Cut bacon into small pieces.

2. Return skillet to medium heat. Add okra and fry until soft. Add tomatoes and cook, stirring, for about 1 minute. Remove from heat.

3. Season with salt and pepper and gently stir in bacon.

Pumpkin Twins

It's time to head to the pumpkin patch and pick out the perfect pumpkin for your porch. But what happens when you see two gourds you want to bring home? You get twin pumpkins!

Pumpkin Twins

- enough cooked rice to fill half a bento box
- 1 or 2 lettuce leaves
- 1 serving Chikuwa Cheese Tempura >
- bento fillers such as cherry tomatoes, sliced cocktail wieners, lightly pickled cucumbers with sesame seeds, or star-shaped fried potatoes
- 2 thick slices boiled carrot
- ½-inch piece green vegetable skin, such as from cucumber or zucchini
- 1 piece nori

1. Fill half of a bento box with rice, using a fork to pat the top flat. Line the other half with lettuce. Place Chikuwa Cheese Tempura on top of lettuce. Tuck in bento fillers.

2. Use a pumpkin cutter to cut 2 shapes out of carrot. Use the tip of a small knife to cut ridges into the pumpkins.

3. With scissors or a sharp knife, cut 2 stems and 2 noses out of green vegetable skin. Place on pumpkins. Cut out 2 green stars for garnish.

4. Use a nori punch and kitchen scissors to create 4 nori eyes and 2 mouths. Apply to pumpkins with a slightly moistened toothpick. Arrange pumpkins on top of rice.

Chikuwa Cheese Tempura
Makes 1 serving

- ½ slice white American cheese
- 1 chikuwa fish cake
- 1 tbsp all-purpose flour
- ½ tbsp ice water
- 1 tsp green laver (seaweed)
- oil for frying

1. Cut cheese into thick matchsticks. Stuff cheese into the hollow center of the chikuwa. Slice chikuwa into bite-sized pieces.

2. Combine flour and ice water in a small bowl and mix gently. Fold in laver. Line a plate with paper towels; set aside.

3. Heat oil in a pan over medium heat. Test the oil to see if it is hot enough for frying: Drop a small amount of batter into it; it should immediately rise to the top. Dip chikuwa pieces in batter and fry until light brown. Transfer to paper-towel-lined plate to drain before serving.

A pumpkin in the hand is worth two in the lunch.

Every Thanksgiving, Americans gather with family and friends to eat lots of yummy foods, especially delicious turkey. The holiday dates all the way back to the early 1600s, when the Pilgrims were the first to celebrate it.

Turkey-Loving Pilgrim

- 1 slice white American cheese
- purple and green food coloring
- 1 slice yellow American cheese
- 1 small piece nori
- dab of ketchup
- 2 slices white bread
- your favorite sandwich fillings
- 1 serving fruit
- 1 side salad

1. With an oval cutter, cut a shape out of white American cheese for the Pilgrim's hat. Use a snowman cutter to cut a body out of white American cheese. Use a knife to cut off the snowman's hat and trim the bottom of the body to make it flat.

2. In a bowl, mix 1 drop purple food coloring and 2 drops green food coloring to make brown. Use a toothpick to paint the lower half of the body brown. Place body on hat.

3. To make a cheese collar: Use snowman cutter to cut another body out of white American cheese. With a knife, cut off head and bottom circle of body, and cut a triangle out of the middle as shown. Place collar on top of the Pilgrim's brown dress.

4. Use a knife to cut bangs and pigtails out of yellow American cheese. Arrange on Pilgrim. If needed, cut a piece out of the hat to insert the pigtails.

5. Use a nori punch or kitchen scissors to cut out nori eyes and a mouth, and place features on face. Dot ketchup onto cheeks with a toothpick.

6. Use a large oval cutter to cut bread. Use a knife to cut off the bottom.

7. Assemble sandwich and arrange Pilgrim on top. Serve with fruit and salad.

This little Pilgrim girl is ready for her feast!

Winter Wonderland

Even though the harvest is over and the snow is starting to fall, winter has strong associations with food. Warm soups and stews become the highlight of the day. Comforting fare such as broccoli, potatoes, and leeks are in season. And holidays like Christmas and Valentine's Day each have special flavors and foods to celebrate.

When winter is here, wear your mittens to prevent frosty fingers. Although this adorable pair won't warm your hands, they will surely warm your heart and brighten your bento lunch.

Pair of Mittens

- ❧ enough cooked rice to fill half a bento box
- ❧ 1 or 2 lettuce leaves
- ❧ 1 serving Stuffed Shiitake Mushrooms ›
- ❧ 1 serving Tuna Spaghetti (see page 135)
- ❧ sprinkle of Parmesan
- ❧ 1 piece baby corn, sliced into rounds
- ❧ 1 edamame bean, peeled and split
- ❧ bento fillers such as steamed broccoli florets or tomatoes
- ❧ 1 slice white American cheese
- ❧ 1 slice salami or ham

1. Fill half of a bento box with rice, using a fork to pat the top flat. Line the other half with lettuce. Arrange Stuffed Shiitake Mushrooms on the lettuce.

2. Twirl a forkful of Tuna Spaghetti and add to the bento box. Sprinkle with Parmesan. Decorate with slices of baby corn and edamame bean. Tuck in bento fillers.

3. Fold cheese in half to create a double layer. Top with salami. With a mitten cutter, cut out 2 stacks of mittens. Flip 1 mitten over so the cheese is on top.

4. Using a heart cutter, cut hearts out of leftover meat and cheese. Place a contrasting heart on each mitten. Use the bottom of the mitten cutter to cut an extra cuff out of meat and cheese. Place cuffs on contrasting mittens.

5. Place mittens on rice. Arrange a leftover Tuna Spaghetti noodle as a string.

Stuffed Shiitake Mushrooms
Makes 2 to 3 servings

- ❧ 1 tbsp bread crumbs
- ❧ 1 tbsp milk
- ❧ 7 oz ground pork
- ❧ 3 tbsp chopped onion
- ❧ 1 quail egg or ¼ chicken egg, beaten
- ❧ pinch of salt
- ❧ pinch of ground black pepper
- ❧ 6 shiitake mushrooms
- ❧ 1 tsp cornstarch
- ❧ oil for sautéing
- ❧ 3 tbsp sake or white wine

1. In a medium bowl, soak bread crumbs in milk until moist, about 1 minute. Add pork, onion, egg, salt, and pepper. Mix well with your hands.

2. Form mixture into round dumplings about the size of the mushrooms. Dust mushrooms with cornstarch, then place dumplings inside mushroom caps.

3. Heat oil in a pan over medium heat. Sauté mushrooms, pork side down, until browned. Flip once and brown on the other side.

4. Add sake to the pan, cover, and let steam for a few minutes, until alcohol is cooked off. Uncover and cook until liquid is gone.

Melting Snowman

This snowman does not mix well with warm hugs.

Uh-oh! This poor little snowman is melting. Fortunately, he's got a few snowflakes to keep him company even with the sun out.

Melting Snowman

- 1 quail egg, hard-boiled but still warm
- enough cooked rice to fill half a bento box
- 1 or 2 lettuce leaves
- 2 pieces Daikon Gyoza (see page 132)
- bento fillers such as sliced boiled okra, broccoli florets, tomatoes, or lemon slices
- 1 thin slice carrot
- 1 small hamburger patty, cooked
- 1 fried spaghetti noodle
- 1 slice swiss cheese
- 1 piece nori
- hat-shaped food pick
- 3 pieces cooked snowflake-shaped pasta

1. Prepare a bowl of ice water. While egg is still warm, peel it and mold into a sphere with your fingers. Chill in ice water for 10 minutes, or until set.

2. Fill half of a bento box with rice, using a fork to pat top flat. Line the other half with lettuce. Place Daikon Gyoza on lettuce and tuck in bento fillers.

3. Cut a snowman's nose from the slice of carrot using a piece of thin drinking straw.

4. Remove egg from water and pat dry. Assemble snowman using egg, hamburger patty, and swiss cheese, as shown below. Attach snowman's nose while cheese is still warm.

5. Use a nori punch and kitchen scissors to create nori eyes, mouth, and buttons. Apply to the cheese. Use remaining spaghetti to make arms.

6. Place a piece of lettuce on rice and top with snowman patty. Press hat pick into the top of the snowman. Garnish with pasta.

How to Melt a Snowman

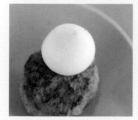

❶ Insert a piece of spaghetti into bottom of egg and press the other end into the hamburger patty. Place on a microwave-safe plate.

❷ Use a large round cutter with a scalloped edge to cut a shape out of swiss cheese. Gently rest cheese on top of quail egg.

❸ Microwave for a few seconds, until cheese has melted over both egg and hamburger.

Smallest Walrus

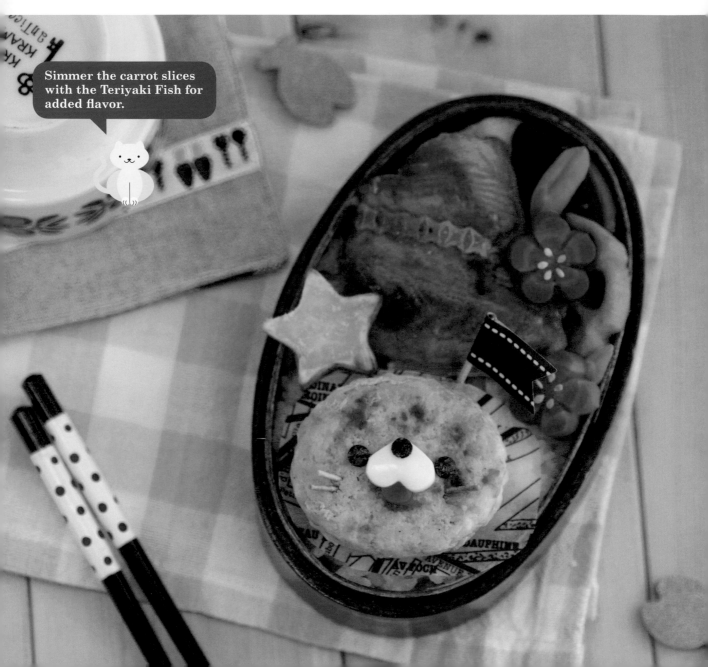

Simmer the carrot slices with the Teriyaki Fish for added flavor.

Although walruses love to lie around, they also like to socialize, which explains why this blubbery little fella looks like he's smiling at you. Walruses live in the Arctic, so be sure to pack him on a bed of (r)ice.

Smallest Walrus

- enough cooked rice to fill half a bento box
- sprinkle of furikake (colored rice seasoning)
- 1 shiso leaf
- Teriyaki Fish ›
- bento fillers such as cooked vegetables
- 3 slices boiled carrot
- 10 sesame seeds
- 1 Tsukune patty (see page 35)
- ⅛ slice white American cheese
- 1 piece nori
- 1 fried spaghetti noodle
- 1 slice boiled and fried sweet potato

1. Fill half of a bento box with rice, using a fork to pat the top flat. Sprinkle with furikake. Place shiso leaf on the edge of the rice. Arrange Teriyaki Fish in the other half of the box. Tuck in bento fillers.

2. With a flower cutter, cut 2 flowers out of carrot. (See page 25 for carrot flower tutorial.) Arrange on Teriyaki Fish. Place sesame seeds in the center of carrot flowers. Place Tsukune meatball on rice.

3. With a piece of thick drinking straw, cut a circle from the remaining carrot slice and place on the patty as the walrus tongue.

4. With a mini heart cutter or a knife, cut out a cheese heart and round off the point to create a walrus snout. (If you don't have a mini heart cutter, use a small flower cutter and remove 2 petals with a knife.) Place snout over the tongue.

5. Use a nori punch to create nori eyes and a nose. Arrange on face. Break fried spaghetti noodle into 4 pieces and insert into patty as whiskers. Arrange walrus on rice, placing a layer of decorative paper underneath to provide contrast, if needed.

6. With a star cutter or knife, cut a shape out of sweet potato. Fry in a little cooking oil until golden brown. Place on rice.

Teriyaki Fish
Makes 1 serving

- 2 oz fish such as yellowtail or salmon
- 1 tbsp sake
- 2 tsp soy sauce
- 1 tsp mirin
- ½ tsp grated fresh ginger
- 1 tsp extra virgin olive oil
- ½ tsp granulated sugar

1. Cut fish into bite-size pieces. In a bowl, combine sake, soy sauce, mirin, and ginger. Add fish and mix to coat. Cover and marinate for 10 minutes.

2. In a sauté pan, heat oil over medium heat. Add fish, reserving marinade, and sauté, flipping once, until golden brown on both sides. Reduce heat and cook on low heat for 5 to 6 minutes, until cooked through.

3. Add sugar to marinade and pour it into the pan. Simmer for 1 to 2 minutes, until thickened.

Polar Bear Pal

Polar bears are one of the largest carnivores on land, and they can travel great distances in search of their next meal. Fortunately, you don't have to do the same—yours is neatly packed and ready to go!

Polar Bear Pal

- 1 cup cooked rice
- 1 package blue decofuri (optional)
- 1 or 2 lettuce leaves
- 1 serving Easy Tandoori Chicken ›
- bento fillers such as broccoli florets or orange slices
- 1 slice white American cheese
- 1 slice ham
- 1 piece nori
- 1 slice boiled or fried potato
- 3 to 5 green peas

1. If dyeing rice blue: In a bowl, mix together rice and decofuri. Fill half of a bento box with rice, using a fork to pat top flat. Line the other half with lettuce and top with Easy Tandoori Chicken and bento fillers.

2. With a bear cutter or toothpick, cut a bear shape out of cheese. With a snowflake cutter, cut a snowflake out of ham and use the bear cutter to cut it in half. Place snowflake on the bear's back, aligning the curve of the bear with the curve of the snowflake.

3. Use a piece of thin drinking straw to punch a nose and cheek out of ham. Place on bear's face.

4. Use a nori punch or scissors to cut out a nori eye and mouth. Apply to bear with a slightly moistened toothpick. Place bear on rice.

5. Cut a snowflake out of potato and arrange on rice. Garnish with peas.

Easy Tandoori Chicken
Makes 2 to 3 servings

- 7 oz boneless, skinless chicken breasts
- 3 tbsp plain yogurt
- ⅓ tsp curry powder
- pinch of chili powder
- pinch of garlic powder
- pinch of salt
- pinch of ground black pepper
- cooking oil

1. Cut chicken into bite-size pieces. In a bowl, combine yogurt, curry powder, chili powder, garlic powder, salt, and pepper. Mix well. Add chicken to bowl and toss to coat. Cover and marinate overnight in the refrigerator.

2. In a sauté pan, heat a bit of oil over medium-high heat. Cook chicken, stirring occasionally, for 5 to 10 minutes, until browned on all sides and cooked through.

Better eat quickly before this polar bear gobbles up all your Tandoori Chicken.

Frosty the Snowman

Makes
1 bento

This bento is a great way to use star-shaped or holiday-themed food picks.

What better way to chase away winter blues than to make a cheery snowman? This adorable tribute to Frosty has a comfy red scarf and a happy red hat that are guaranteed to make you smile.

Frosty the Snowman

- 1 or 2 lettuce leaves
- 2 rice balls (see page 132)
- 1 serving Fried Pork and Vegetables >
- bento fillers such as okra, tomatoes, or boiled asparagus
- 1 slice kamaboko, hanpen fish cake, or boiled potato
- 1 stick imitation crab (kanikama)
- 1 piece nori
- 1 boiled green bean or asparagus stalk
- 1 slice boiled rose potato or purple potato
- cooking oil

1. Line a bento box with lettuce. Place rice balls on lettuce. Arrange Fried Pork and Vegetables in bento box. Tuck in bento fillers.

2. With an oval cutter, cut a shape out of kamaboko for Frosty's body. With a knife, cut scarf and hat shapes out of imitation crab. Secure hat to snowman's body with a toothpick. Arrange scarf around neck.

3. Use a nori punch or kitchen scissors to create nori eyes, mouth, and buttons. Apply to Frosty with a slightly moistened toothpick. Use a piece of small drinking straw to cut a red nose out of leftover imitation crab and place on face. Place Frosty on one rice ball.

4. Slice green bean into 7 to 9 small pieces. Arrange them in a wreath on the other rice ball. Use a mini star cutter to cut a star out of leftover imitation crab. Place it on wreath.

5. Use a star cutter or knife to cut a star out of rose potato. Heat a little oil in a small sauté pan over medium heat. Add potato and cook until lightly browned. Garnish bento with potato star.

Fried Pork and Vegetables
Makes 1 serving

- 1½ oz thinly sliced pork
- 1 tsp cornstarch
- oil for frying
- 1½ oz green pepper, julienned
- 2 oz carrot, julienned
- pinch of salt
- pinch of ground black pepper
- 2 tsp sake or white wine
- a few dashes of soy sauce

1. Dredge pork in cornstarch. Heat oil in a sauté pan over medium heat. Add pepper and carrot and cook for about 4 minutes, until softened. Remove from heat and set aside.

2. Add pork to pan and cook for about 2 minutes, until crispy. Return vegetables to pan.

3. Season with salt and pepper. Add sake and cook for 1 to 2 minutes, until liquid is evaporated. Sprinkle with soy sauce.

Gingerbread Friends

Run, run, as fast as you can! Can you catch two gingerbread men? They look mischievous but happy as they frolic through your lunchtime.

Gingerbread Friends

- enough cooked rice to fill half a bento box
- 1 or 2 lettuce leaves
- 1 serving Chicken Katsu >
- bento fillers such as sliced green beans or pickled tomatoes
- 1 slice SPAM
- 1 tsp yellow mustard
- 1 tsp brown sugar
- 1 piece nori
- ¼ slice white American cheese

1. Preheat toaster oven to low and line a tray with aluminum foil.

2. Fill half of a bento box with rice, using a fork to pat the top flat. Line the other half with lettuce. Arrange Chicken Katsu on lettuce. Tuck in bento fillers.

3. With a mini body cutter, cut 2 gingerbread men out of SPAM. In a small bowl, combine mustard and brown sugar. Place gingerbread men on foil-lined tray and spread mustard mixture evenly on them. Transfer to toaster oven and cook, watching carefully so sauce doesn't burn, until sauce is golden and bubbly. Set aside to cool.

4. Use a nori punch or kitchen scissors to create nori eyes and mouths. Apply to gingerbread men using a slightly moistened toothpick.

5. Use a piece of thin drinking straw to cut 4 circles out of cheese. Once the gingerbread men have cooled, place 2 circles on each body. Arrange gingerbread men on top of the rice.

Chicken Katsu
Makes 1 serving

- oil for frying
- 1 boneless, skinless chicken thigh
- pinch of salt
- pinch of ground black pepper
- 1 tbsp all-purpose flour
- 1 egg, beaten
- ½ cup panko
- katsu sauce for serving

1. In a small pan, add enough oil to cover the bottom and place over medium-high heat. Line a plate with paper towels.

2. Cut chicken into bite-size pieces. Season with salt and pepper.

3. Place flour in a small bowl, egg in a second, and panko in a third. Dredge chicken in flour, dip in egg, and coat in panko. Then dip in egg again and coat in another layer of panko.

4. Place chicken in oil and fry, flipping once, until golden brown on both sides. Transfer to the paper-towel-lined plate to drain. Serve warm with katsu sauce.

Pack katsu sauce in a small sauce bottle or packet. Put it on the chicken when you're ready to eat.

Tomato Santas

Cute food doesn't have to be made for a bento lunch. These little tomato Santas make adorably festive hors d'oeuvres. Delight your coworkers at the holiday party with these fluffy, tasty snacks.

Tomato Santas

- 3 cherry or grape tomatoes
- ½ cup Mashed Potatoes >
- 1 piece nori

1. Cut tomatoes in half. Remove pulp from the bottom half and drain both halves of juice and seeds. Use a piece of drinking straw to punch out 3 noses from tomato pulp.

2. Attach a piping tip to a pastry bag and fill bag with mashed potatoes. Pipe potatoes into bottom halves of tomatoes. Arrange tops of tomatoes as hats.

3. Use a nori punch to make eyes and use a slightly moistened toothpick to adhere them to potatoes. Place tomato noses between nori eyes.

4. Pipe mashed potato pom-poms onto the tops of the tomato hats.

Making dessert? Substitute strawberries and whipped cream for the tomatoes and mashed potatoes. Use sprinkles and nonpareils for the facial features!

Mashed Potatoes
Makes enough for 10 Santas

- 1 medium-sized potato, boiled or steamed, peeled, and roughly chopped
- 1½ tbsp heavy cream, plus more if needed
- pinch of salt
- pinch of ground black pepper

1. Pass potatoes through a potato ricer or mash with a potato masher. Add cream, salt, and pepper. Mix well.

2. Add more cream if mashed potato is difficult to pipe.

❀ Cut a grape tomato in half diagonally and use a toothpick to attach the halves like a stocking. You may want to cut the top to make it flat. Trim your stocking with white American cheese and decorate it with tomato pieces and parsley sprigs.

Penguin Elves

When the holiday season arrives, Santa needs lots of help. This year he had to recruit some penguins from all the way at the South Pole to help make enough toys for the Nice List.

Penguin Elves

- 1 fried tofu skin (*aburaage*)
- 1 tbsp soy sauce, plus extra for seasoning
- 1 tbsp sake
- 1 tbsp granulated sugar
- 1 sheet nori
- 2 rice balls (see page 132)
- 1 or 2 lettuce leaves
- Chikuwa Cheese Tempura (see page 101)
- bento fillers such as broccoli florets, tomatoes, or boiled choy sum leaves seasoned with soy sauce
- 1 piece uncooked spaghetti noodle
- 4 corn kernels

1. Bring a pot of water to a boil. Use tongs to dip tofu skin into boiling water to rinse excess oil. Pat dry with paper towel. Cut tofu skin in half diagonally to form 2 triangles.

2. In a small saucepan, bring soy sauce, sake, sugar, and ¾ cup water to a boil. Add tofu skins. Simmer uncovered for 10 minutes, or until the liquid has evaporated.

3. Use a sharp knife to cut penguin face markings out of nori. Wrap nori around rice balls.

4. Line a bento box with lettuce.

5. Wrap tofu skins around the tops of the penguins as elf hats. Arrange in bento box. Fill remaining spaces with Chikuwa Cheese Tempura and bento fillers.

6. With a nori punch, cut out 4 nori eyes and add them to the penguins. Insert a small piece of spaghetti into the back of each corn kernel. Pin them onto the penguins to form beaks.

Fold the nori sheet in half to cut out two penguin faces at once.

Rudolph the Red-Nosed Bagel

Makes
1 sandwich

This bagel is ready to help Santa pull his sleigh through the harsh blizzard to get toys to sleeping children around the world. With a red nose and hooves covering his grin of glee, Rudolph can't believe how lucky he is!

Reindeer Bagel

- 1 bagel
- 1 egg, hard-boiled
- 1 tbsp chopped celery (optional)
- 1 tbsp mayonnaise
- salt to taste
- ground black pepper to taste
- 1 lettuce leaf
- 1 slice tomato
- bento fillers such as tomatoes or cucumber
- ½ slice yellow American cheese
- ¼ slice white American cheese
- holiday food picks (optional)
- 2 slices boiled potato
- 1 cocktail wiener
- 1 cherry tomato, halved
- 1 piece nori

1. Slice bagel in half and toast until lightly golden. In a small bowl, mince egg with a fork. Add celery (if using), mayonnaise, salt, and pepper. Mix well. On one bagel half, stack lettuce, tomato slice, and egg salad. Top with other bagel half and place in a bento box.

2. Tuck in bento fillers. With a star cutter, cut shapes out of both cheese slices. Garnish bento with cheese stars and food picks, if using.

3. With an airplane cutter or a knife, cut 2 airplanes (antlers) out of potato slices; if using airplanes, remove one wing from each. Heat a small sauté pan over medium heat. Add potato slices and fry until golden brown. Insert into the top of the sandwich as antlers.

4. With a piece of thick drinking straw, cut eyes out of remaining white cheese. With a nori punch, cut 2 smaller circles as pupils and place on cheese. Place eyes on bagel.

5. Cut 2 thin round slices of cocktail wiener and place on bagel as cheeks. Cut off a 1-inch piece from one end of the wiener and slice in half lengthwise. Cut triangle notches out of the ends to create hooves. Attach to bagel.

6. Place one half of the cherry tomato in the center of the bagel as a nose. With a knife, cut a mouth and a small diamond out of remaining yellow cheese. Place mouth on bagel and diamond on nose as a sparkle.

7. With a circle cutter, cut a shape out of remaining cheese. With a knife, cut circle in half. Tuck the halves into the top of the sandwich near the antlers as ears.

Mr. and Mrs. Claus

Everyone has a favorite chili recipe—vegetarian chili, white chili, chili verde, even canned chili. Whether served for a football game, a winter potluck, or just a frigid afternoon, this hearty dish is sure to warm you up. But what to do with the leftovers? Dress them up with Mr. and Mrs. Claus hot dogs!

Mr. and Mrs. Claus

- enough cooked rice to fill half a bento box
- enough leftover chili to fill half a bento box
- sprinkle of grated Parmesan cheese
- 1 hot dog, boiled
- 1 slice white American cheese
- 1 grape tomato, halved widthwise
- 1 piece nori
- 1 piece ham or salami
- 2 or 3 boiled snow peas
- 1 slice boiled carrot

1. Fill half of a bento box with rice. Fill the other half with chili. Sprinkle chili with Parmesan to look like snow.

2. Cut a 2-inch piece off one rounded end of the hot dog for Mrs. Claus. Cut a 1½-inch piece of hot dog for Santa. With a knife, cut out a square of cheese for Mrs. Claus's apron, and then cut out a smaller square as a collar. Wrap around the wiener with the rounded end.

3. Tuck both hot dogs into the chili with the flat ends pressed into the rice. With a cloud cutter, cut a cloud out of cheese. Use the round edge of another cutter to cut off one end, creating Santa's beard. Place on Santa.

4. With a knife, cut a strip of cheese and wrap it around the bottom of one tomato half as trim.

Place hat on Santa's head and secure with a toothpick. With a piece of large drinking straw or a circle cutter, cut out a small circle of cheese and use it to top Santa's hat.

5. Use a toothpick to cut out Mrs. Claus's hair and bun. Place on her head and secure with a toothpick.

6. With a piece of thin drinking straw, cut out a cheese nose and add to Santa's face. Use a nori punch or kitchen scissors to cut eyes and mouths. Apply to faces.

7. Stack ham on cheese and use a knife to cut out rectangular or square presents. With a knife or kitchen scissors, cut out 4 nori strips and 2 nori hearts. Place strips in a crisscross pattern on the presents. Top each with a nori heart as a bow. Place presents on rice.

8. Using the pointed end of a petal cutter, cut out 6 pieces from the snow pea. Layer pea slices like a Christmas tree next to Mrs. Claus. Using a mini star cutter, cut out carrot stars and use them to garnish chili.

No time like the "presents" for lunch!

New Year's Kimono

In Japan today, the kimono is rarely worn; it's most often reserved for special occasions such as weddings or graduations. But one time of the year you're certain to see them is New Year's Day. This little girl is wearing her traditional kimono to celebrate the coming of the new year.

New Year's Kimono

- 1 quail egg, hard-boiled but still warm
- enough cooked rice to fill half a bento box
- 1 or 2 lettuce leaves
- 1 serving Chicken and Veggie Stir-Fry >
- 1 piece Grilled Satoimo (see page 135)
- bento fillers such as boiled broccoli florets
- 1 piece nori
- 1 cocktail wiener or boiled baby carrot
- food pick
- black sesame seeds
- dab of ketchup

1. Prepare a bowl of ice water. Peel warm quail egg and shape it into a sphere with your fingers. Chill in ice water for 5 to 10 minutes. Drain.

2. Fill half of a bento box with rice, using a fork to pat the top flat. Line the other half with lettuce. Fill lettuce with Chicken and Veggie Stir-Fry, Grilled Satoimo, and bento fillers.

3. With kitchen scissors, cut 3 thin nori strips. Wrap 2 around quail egg to create a bob haircut for the girl. If necessary, moisten nori with a bit of water to help it stick to the egg.

4. Cut rounded ends off wiener to make the girl's body. Use a food pick to attach head to body. Place on rice.

5. Use tweezers to place sesame seeds as eyes. With a knife, cut a tiny mouth out of leftover wiener. Use a toothpick to dab ketchup on cheeks. Wrap third nori strip around her body as a sash.

Chicken and Veggie Stir-Fry
Makes 1 serving

- 1 oz boneless, skinless chicken breast
- cooking oil
- ¼ maitake mushroom, chopped
- ⅛ small red bell pepper, chopped
- ⅛ small yellow pepper, chopped
- 1 tsp sake or cooking wine
- 1 tsp Thai fish sauce
- salt to taste
- ground black pepper to taste

1. Cut chicken breast into bite-size pieces. In a sauté pan, heat oil over medium heat. Add chicken and stir-fry for about 3 or 4 minutes, until lightly browned on both sides.

2. Add mushrooms and peppers. Stir for about 30 seconds. Add sake, fish sauce, salt, and pepper. Stir until vegetables are cooked through.

Finish your kimono girl with a food pick decorated to symbolize *kanzashi*, or Japanese hair ornaments!

All Dressed Up

Especially for you

The way to a man's heart is through his lunchbox.

Winter offers plenty of chances to don fancy clothes, from a winter wedding on Valentine's Day to an unforgettable New Year's Eve. This bento is all formal attire with a tuxedo and ball gown.

Formal Hearts

- enough cooked rice to fill half a bento box
- 1 or 2 lettuce leaves
- 1 serving Fried Shrimp with Broccoli ›
- small handful of spinach
- salt to taste
- sprinkle of bonito flakes
- bento fillers such as boiled broccoli or tomatoes
- bow-shaped food picks, optional
- ½ slice white American cheese
- ¼ piece hanpen fish cake, kamaboko, or sweet potato
- 1 piece nori
- ¼ slice ham
- 2 kidney beans

1. Fill half of a bento box with rice, using a fork to pat the top flat. Line the other half with lettuce. Arrange Fried Shrimp with Broccoli on lettuce.

2. In a small pot of boiling water, cook spinach until softened and wilted. Drain well and toss with salt. Tuck into bento box next to shrimp and broccoli, and top with bonito flakes. Tuck in bento fillers and decorative food picks.

3. Stack cheese on fish cake. With a heart cutter, cut out 2 stacks. Use kitchen scissors to cut a nori tuxedo shape and bow tie. Apply to one stack.

4. Use a heart cutter to cut a heart out of ham. Move cutter up and trim off some of the bottom of the heart to create the ball gown. Place on the other stack. Use a piece of thin drinking straw to cut a gem from remaining cheese; place on ball gown.

5. Place both hearts on rice. Cut the kidney beans on a diagonal. Arrange into mini hearts and add to bento box.

Fried Shrimp with Broccoli
Makes 2 servings

- 4 medium-size shrimp, peeled and deveined
- 1 tbsp cornstarch
- 1 tbsp sesame oil
- ¼ tsp minced fresh ginger
- 2 or 3 boiled broccoli florets
- pinch of salt
- 1 tbsp sake or white wine
- dash of soy sauce

1. Pat shrimp dry with paper towels. In a plastic zip-top bag, toss shrimp with cornstarch.

2. In a small pan, heat oil over medium heat. Add ginger and cook for about 30 seconds, until fragrant. Add shrimp and stir-fry for about 2 minutes, until it turns pink.

3. Add broccoli, salt, and sake. Cover and simmer for 2 minutes. Sprinkle with soy sauce.

Valentine Bear

Just in time for Valentine's Day, this pink bear is smitten! He can't take his gaze off of his sweetheart. You can see it in his eyes.

Valentine Bear

- 1 cup steamed rice, dyed pink (see page 16)
- 1 or 2 lettuce leaves
- 1 serving Teriyaki Beef >
- bento fillers such as okra, tomatoes, corn, or broccoli
- 1 slice sweet potato or potato
- cooking oil
- 1 slice boiled carrot
- 1 green pea
- 1 piece nori

1. Shape rice into 1 large ball for a face and 2 smaller balls for ears.

2. Line a bento box with lettuce. Place large rice ball on lettuce and ears above it. Arrange Teriyaki Beef in bento box. Tuck in bento fillers.

3. With a heart cutter, cut 2 shapes out of sweet potato. In a small sauté pan over medium heat, warm a little oil. Cook potatoes, flipping once, until golden brown. Place 1 heart on the bear's face as its snout.

4. Use a piece of drinking straw to cut 2 carrot circles for cheeks. Place next to bear's snout and add green pea as a nose.

5. Fold nori in half and cut out 2 half hearts along the fold to make 2 hearts. Add as eyes. Garnish with the second potato heart.

Teriyaki Beef
Makes 4 servings

- ½ cup dark soy sauce
- ½ cup granulated sugar
- 1 tsp minced garlic
- ½ tsp grated fresh ginger
- 1 lb thinly sliced beef
- 1 tbsp butter

1. In a large bowl, combine soy sauce, sugar, ½ cup water, garlic, and ginger. Add beef and mix well. Cover and marinate in the refrigerator for at least 30 minutes.

2. In a skillet over medium-high heat, melt butter. Add beef and sauté for 5 to 7 minutes, until cooked through and nicely browned. Do not char meat.

For even more love, cut tamagoyaki (page 37) in half on a diagonal and rearrange the pieces to make a heart.

Additional Recipes

Here are some tasty bento-friendly recipes you may want to pack in one of your boxes!

Rice Ball (Onigiri)
Makes 1 rice ball

- about ⅓ cup cooked rice, still warm
- a few pinches of salt
- 1 piece nori (optional)

1. Sprinkle rice with salt. With a rice paddle mix together to combine and cool.

2. Scoop rice onto a piece of plastic wrap. Wrap rice with plastic, forming it into a ball, triangle, oval, or other shape. The plastic helps shape the rice and keeps it from sticking to your hands.

3. Unwrap rice ball. Wrap with nori (if using). If necessary, dab a bit of water on nori to help it stick to the rice. Make onigiri as needed; if prepared in advance, they will dry out.

Pork Mushroom Roll
Makes 2 rolls

- 1 small eryngi mushroom (also known as king oyster mushroom)
- 2 pieces thinly sliced pork chop
- pinch of salt
- pinch of ground black pepper
- oil for frying

1. Cut mushroom into quarters.

2. Roll 2 mushroom slices in each piece of pork. Secure the ends with toothpicks. Sprinkle with salt and pepper.

3. In a small sauté pan, heat oil over medium heat. Place pork rolls in pan, seam side down, and sauté for 3 to 4 minutes, flipping once, until pork is golden brown and mushrooms begin to soften.

Beef and Sweet Potato Rolls
Makes 2 rolls

- 2 ¼-inch-thick slices boiled sweet potato
- 2 or 3 thin slices beef
- ½ tsp grated fresh ginger
- 1 tsp granulated sugar
- 1 tsp soy sauce
- 1 tsp sake
- oil for cooking

1. Cut sweet potatoes into thick matchsticks. Wrap with beef slices and secure with toothpicks.

2. In a small bowl, combine ginger, sugar, soy sauce, and sake. Mix well.

3. Heat oil in a sauté pan over medium heat. Sauté rolls until lightly browned. Add ginger mixture and simmer until cooked through.

Daikon Gyoza
Makes 20 dumplings

- ¼ cup finely chopped daikon
- 3 oz ground pork
- ½ tsp grated fresh ginger
- ½ tsp soy sauce
- 20 thin slices daikon, about 3 inches in diameter
- ½ tsp salt
- 1 tbsp cornstarch
- oil for frying

1. In a bowl, combine chopped daikon, pork, ginger, and soy sauce. Mix well.

2. Place sliced daikon in a bowl and sprinkle with salt. Let stand for 5 minutes, or until soft. Drain and dry daikon with paper towels.

3. Place sliced daikon on a plate or work surface and sprinkle with cornstarch.

4. Place 2 to 3 tsp. filling in the center of each slice. Fold daikon around filling to seal dumplings.

5. Heat oil in a pan over medium heat. Fry gyoza until golden brown on both sides.

Lemon Salted Fried Chicken
Makes 4 to 5 servings

- 1 tbsp lemon juice
- 1 tbsp olive oil
- 2 tsp salt
- ground black pepper to taste
- 10 ounces boneless chicken breast, fat removed, cut into bite-size pieces
- 3 tbsp cornstarch
- a few half slices sweet potato
- a few tbsp oil for frying

1. In a bowl, combine lemon juice, olive oil, salt, and black pepper. Add chicken and toss to coat. Cover and marinate for at least 30 minutes.

2. Drain chicken, discarding marinade, and dust with cornstarch. In a skillet, heat oil over medium-high heat. Fry chicken until golden brown and cooked through. Drain on paper towels.

3. Fry sweet potato slices until cooked through.

Tuna Patties
Makes 6 to 8 large patties

- 1 7-oz can tuna, drained
- 1 egg
- 1 small potato, boiled and mashed
- ½ stalk celery, minced
- 1 scallion, minced
- 1 handful cilantro leaves, minced (optional)
- 1 tsp chicken bouillon
- ¼ tsp garlic salt
- salt to taste
- ½ to 1 tbsp cooking oil

1. Mix together all ingredients except oil. Taste and season as needed. With your hands form mixture into 6 to 8 patties.

2. Heat oil in a large pan over medium heat. Line a plate with paper towels. Sauté patties for 2 to 3 minutes on each side, or until nicely browned.

3. Transfer patties to the paper-towel-lined plate. Let cool and then slice into pieces that can fit in a bento box.

Beef and Kimchi Stir-Fry
Makes 1 to 2 servings

- a few tbsp sesame oil
- 2 oz thinly sliced beef, cut into strips
- 1 tbsp kimchi, roughly chopped
- 1 tsp thinly sliced scallions
- 1 slice carrot, chopped
- 4 or 5 frozen green peas
- pinch of ground black pepper
- ½ tsp black sesame seeds

1. In a small pan, heat oil over medium-high heat. Add beef and stir-fry for 30 seconds.

2. Add kimchi, scallions, and carrot. Stir-fry for about 2 minutes, until cooked through.

3. Sprinkle with peas, pepper, and sesame seeds. Cook just until peas turn bright green.

Garlic Green Beans
Makes 1 serving

- 1 tsp olive oil
- ½ tsp minced garlic
- 2 or 3 fresh green beans, cut into 1-inch pieces

1. Heat oil in a small pan over medium-high heat. Add garlic and cook for about 30 seconds. Add green beans and stir-fry until bright green.

2. Remove from pan and set aside to cool. Beans should be slightly tender but crunchy.

Garlic Chicken
Makes 4 servings

- ½ cup light soy sauce
- ½ cup granulated sugar
- 4 tbsp minced garlic, divided
- 1 tbsp sesame seeds
- 2 tsp sesame oil
- 1 lb boneless chicken thighs
- ½ tsp salt
- ground black pepper
- ¼ cup plus 1 tbsp cornstarch, divided
- oil for frying
- ¾ cup all-purpose flour

1. In a small saucepan over medium heat, bring soy sauce, sugar, 3 tablespoons of the garlic, sesame seeds, and sesame oil to a gentle boil. Lower heat and stir for about 10 minutes, until sugar is dissolved and sauce has thickened. Set aside to cool.

2. Cut chicken into bite-size pieces, removing as much fat as possible. Season with salt, pepper, and the remaining 1 tablespoon garlic. Dissolve 1 tablespoon of the cornstarch in 2 tablespoons water, add chicken, and soak for 10 minutes. Drain liquid.

3. Add a few tablespoons of the garlic sauce to the chicken and let marinate for another 10 minutes. Meanwhile, in a wok or pan over medium-high heat, warm enough oil to cover chicken pieces.

4. Combine flour, the remaining ¼ cup cornstarch, and a dash of salt and pepper. Dust chicken pieces in flour mixture and add to wok. Deep-fry chicken for about 10 to 12 minutes, until golden brown and cooked through. Transfer to a wire rack to drain.

5. In a bowl, toss together chicken and the remaining garlic sauce to coat.

Chinese Egg Rolls
Makes 10 egg rolls

- cooking oil for sautéing and frying
- 5 oz ground or thinly sliced pork
- ¼ cup thinly sliced or grated carrots
- 1 oz cooked rice vermicelli noodles
- ½ cup shredded cabbage
- 1 oz thinly sliced Chinese leek
- 1 tbsp chicken stock or other soup stock
- 1 tbsp sesame oil

- 1 tbsp sake or cooking sherry
- 1 tsp soy sauce
- 1 tsp oyster sauce
- several pinches of ground black pepper
- 10 egg roll wrappers
- 1 tbsp cornstarch

1. In a sauté pan heat cooking oil over medium heat. Sauté pork, carrot, noodles, cabbage, and leeks until cooked through.

2. In a small bowl, combine stock, sesame oil, sake, soy sauce, oyster sauce, and pepper. Add to pan. Cook, stirring, until almost all liquid is gone. Drain off remaining liquid.

3. Lay out an egg roll wrapper with one corner facing you and add filling near the bottom corner. Do not overfill.

4. Roll wrapper and filling away from you halfway up the wrapper, and then fold sides in toward the center. Continue rolling, tucking in any loose spots to ensure a tight roll.

5. Combine cornstarch with 1 tablespoon water. Dip your fingers in cornstarch slurry and moisten the top corner of the wrapper to seal the roll. Place roll on a plate with the corner seam facing down. Repeat with remaining filling and wrappers. If stacking rolls, separate layers with parchment or wax paper to prevent sticking.

6. In a sauté pan, heat cooking oil over medium-high heat. Add egg rolls and fry, turning occasionally, until golden brown.

Tuna Spaghetti
Makes 1 to 2 servings

- 1 oz uncooked spaghetti
- pat of butter
- ½ garlic clove, minced
- 1 tbsp canned tuna, drained
- 1 tsp soy sauce
- ground black pepper to taste

1. Cook spaghetti according to package directions until al dente. Drain well. Set aside to cool.

2. In a small pan over medium heat, melt butter. Add garlic. Cook until fragrant.

3. Add tuna and spaghetti and stir for 30 seconds to 1 minute. Add soy sauce and pepper.

Grilled Satoimo
Makes 1 serving

- 1 frozen satoimo (taro root) or small potato
- ½ cup dashi or chicken broth
- cooking spray
- 1 tsp mayonnaise
- 1 tbsp grated cheese
- pinch of minced fresh parsley

1. Preheat a toaster over on the toast setting. Spray a piece of aluminum foil with cooking spray; set aside. In a small pan over medium heat, simmer satoimo with dashi until soft. Drain and transfer to prepared foil.

2. Coat satoimo with mayonnaise. Sprinkle with cheese and parsley. Transfer to toaster oven and toast until cheese is golden brown.

Frozen Fruit Salad
Makes 1 serving

- ¼ cup frozen strawberries
- ¼ cup frozen peaches
- ¼ cup frozen pineapple or mango
- ¼ cup frozen berries
- 3 tablespoons condensed milk

1. Let fruit thaw at room temperature for about 10 minutes. Chop it into small pieces. Place in a bowl, add condensed milk, and mix well. Divide into mini silicone cups on a tray and freeze until set.

2. Store frozen in a container or plastic bag. If serving in a bento box, place into box in the morning so that fruit will be ready to eat by lunchtime.

Cream Corn Croquettes
Makes 4 to 5 croquettes

- 1 tbsp butter
- ⅓ cup minced onion
- 5 tbsp all-purpose flour, divided
- 1 7-oz can corn, with liquid reserved
- ½ cup milk
- pinch of salt
- oil for frying

1. In a pan over medium heat, melt butter. Add onion and sauté until soft. Add 2 tablespoons of the flour and cook until incorporated. Add corn, milk, salt, and pepper. Cook until thickened.

2. Remove pan from heat and spread mixture in a shallow dish. Cool in refrigerator. Meanwhile, place flour in a small bowl, egg in a second, and panko in a third.

3. With your fingers form mixture into 4 or 5 flat dumplings. Dust with flour, dip in egg, and coat with panko.

4. In a pan, heat oil over medium-high heat. Fry croquettes until golden brown on all sides. Drain a wire rack.

Basic Teriyaki Sauce
Makes about 1½ cups

- 1 cup soy sauce
- ½ cup sugar, plus more to taste
- ¼ cup mirin
- 1 tbsp minced garlic
- ½ tbsp grated fresh ginger

Combine ingredients and mix well.

Resources

Want to expand your bento collection? Check out these websites—some old and some new—to see what they have to offer!

Akazuki (www.akazuki.com): A Japanese goods store that ships worldwide, Akazuki has bento-making supplies and accessories as well as bento boxes, furoshiki, and tableware.

Amazon.com (amazon.com, amazon.co.uk): The mega online retailer stocks hundreds of bento boxes, accessories, and specialty Asian groceries.

Bento&Co (www.bentoandco.com): A high-end bento retailer based in France, Bento&Co offers only the top brands of premium bento boxes and elegant bento accessories. Ships worldwide.

Bento Crazy (bentocrazy.ecrater.com): This online shop offers affordable bento accessories as well as cute character bento boxes.

Bentoland (www.bentoland.com.au): This online retailer in Australian ships worldwide and stocks everything from bento boxes to adult tiffins to kid-friendly lunch boxes.

Bentology (www.bentology.net): Formerly known as Laptop Lunches, this company sells modular bento boxes great for helping adults with portion control.

Bentgo (www.bentgo.com): A new bento box company founded in 2013, Bentgo has both adult and kid-specific lunch boxes.

Bento Store (www.bentostore.com.br): Bento makers in Brazil can purchase Mon Bento boxes and high-end accessories.

Bento USA (www.bentousa.com): Creator of the Cute-Z-Cute sandwich cutters, Bento USA offers $6 flat-rate shipping to the continental United States and will also ship worldwide.

Carla Craft (www.carlacraft-hobby.com): Based in Hong Kong, this craft punch company makes high-quality nori punches in various sizes. They ship worldwide via Federal Express only, so combining shipping with friends is advised.

CasaBento (www.casabento.com): Arguably the largest online bento retailer in Europe, CasaBento and offers a huge selection of traditional and modern bento boxes.

Daiso Japan (www.daisojapan.com): Daiso sells bento boxes and some accessories in bulk.

Easy Lunchboxes (www.easylunchboxes.com): An affordable lunch box container system, this California-based company offers a set of four colors for only $13.95 plus shipping.

eBay (www.ebay.com): eBay is still a great place to get bento boxes and accessories, particularly specialty cutters and punches found only in Japan. Shipping policies vary by seller.

ECO Lunchbox (www.ecolunchboxes.com): ECO Lunchbox is dedicated to helping families go plastic-free with a wide variety of metal bento boxes and cloth lunch bags.

Etsy (www.etsy.com): Hands down the best place to get handcrafted items such as bento bags, furoshiki, and bento-themed miniatures, Etsy is a wonderful place to shop for gifts.

Fun Bites (www.funbites.com): Home of the award-winning sandwich cutter, Fun Bites offers several durable food cutters to help create bite-sized fun for young children.

Goodbyn (www.goodbyn.com): Featuring a special lunch box design for kids, Goodbyn offers colorful options of their "Bynto" box.

Grub2Go (www.grub2go.net): This newly launched company makes just one design so far, an elegant bento box with a wooden lid.

Happy Tiffin (www.happytiffin.com): An ecofriendly food container company, Happy Tiffin offers old-style tiffin lunch storage.

J-Box (www.jbox.com): This Japan/San Diego-based company offers a wide variety of bento boxes, accessories, and kitchen supplies.

Japan Centre (www.japancentre.com): This online store offers everything from Japanese foods to bento boxes. They ship to the United Kingdom and Europe.

Life without Plastic (www.lifewithoutplastic. com): Stocking high-quality, ethically sourced, earth-friendly alternatives to plastic, this Canadian company offers a wide variety of wood, stainless-steel, and stoneware goods.

Little Bento World (www.littlebentoworld. com): Based in Australia, this online retailer sells lunch boxes and cute bento accessories.

Lock & Lock (www.locknlock-usa.com): Lock & Lock offers bento lunch box sets along with matching lunch bags.

LunchBots (www.lunchbots.com): Offering stainless-steel bento containers with colorful silicone tops, LunchBots also carries insulated food jars and leakproof containers.

Luv Bento (www.luvbento.com): An online bento store based in western Australia, Luv Bento stocks bento boxes, Japanese kitchenware, and bento accessories.

Marukai (www.marukaiestore.com): At the online store for Marukai, a Japanese market, you can find everything from Japanese foods such as dried soups and rice condiments to cooking tools.

Michaels (www.michaels.com): Craft stores are a great place to pick up craft punches for nori, washi tape for DIY food picks, and baking supplies that can easily double as bento accessories.

Pasta Shoppe (www.pastashoppe.com): This retailer offers a wide variety of pasta in special shapes, themes, and flavors.

Rakuten International (global.rakuten.com/ en/): This online shopping mall is like a Japanese Amazon.com. The store offers a wide variety of products, including bento boxes and accessories.

Reuse It (www.reuseit.com): Stocking a wide variety of stainless steel, plastic, and silicone products, this online store has a large inventory of bento boxes, lunch bags, napkins, and utensils.

Tupperware (www.tupperware.com): Sealable plastic containers are a durable alternative to classic bento boxes. These containers also work very well for storing or freezing leftovers.

Williams-Sonoma (www.williams-sonoma. com): A high-end kitchen store, Williams-Sonoma is a haven for bento enthusiasts looking to expand their kitchen tool and accessory collections.

Yumbox (www.yumboxlunch.com): Yumbox offers leak-proof separated lunch boxes in a wide variety of fun, kid-friendly colors.

Glossary

Here are some common Japanese and Hawaiian bento terms.

aburaage: fried tofu skin, plain or seasoned

black sesame seeds: roasted sesame seeds

bonito flakes: flavored fish flakes, used as light topping on side dishes

chikuwa: a Japanese tube-shaped fish cake

croquette: a small fried dumpling usually made with mashed potatoes, meat, or veggies and coated in panko

daikon: white radish, often pickled or grated for tempura sauce

dashi: soup stock made from seaweed or shrimp

dashimaki tamago: Japanese rolled egg omelet flavored with dashi

decofuri: colored sets of furikake used to tint rice

edamame: soy beans

fish sausage: a bright pink sausage made of fish

furikake: rice seasoning available in a variety of flavors; one very popular flavor is nori komi

green laver: a type of seaweed used as seasoning; also known as *aonori*

gyoza: a Japanese dumpling usually stuffed with pork and vegetables

hana ebi: Hawaiian shrimp powder, available in red or green; used in sushi

hana osushi no moto: plum vinegar powder, used as seasoning and to color rice bright pink

hanpen fish cake: a pure white fish cake that comes in squares

inarizushi: simmered aburaage stuffed with sushi rice or noodles

kamaboko: a firm fish cake usually colored white and pink; used in hot noodle dishes

kanikama: imitation crab stick

karaage: Japanese-style fried chicken

katsu: meat cutlets, usually chicken or pork, breaded with panko

maitake: a mushroom variety also known as hen-of-the-woods

makizushi: rolled sushi with fillings such as meat and veggies

memmi sauce: noodle soup base (*mentsuyu* in Japan) used to make broths and sauces

mirin: sweet rice wine used in cooking

mochiko flour: sweet rice flour

musubi: a rice ball wrapped in nori

nikumaki: vegetables wrapped in thin cutlets and fried

nori: dried seaweed, available in sheets

onigiri: salted rice ball

panko: Japanese-style bread crumbs

rice vinegar: vinegar made from fermented rice

satoimo: taro root

sake: rice wine

seasoned rice vinegar: rice vinegar ready-made for sushi

shiitake mushroom: a Japanese variety of mushroom

shimeji mushroom: Asian variety of mushroom

soba: a thin, brown noodle made from buckwheat

somen: a thin, white noodle made from wheat

soy paper: an alternative to nori; available in a variety of bright colors

sweet chili sauce: a sweet Thai sauce also known as *nam chim kai*

tamagoyaki: Japanese rolled egg omelet

tandoori: an Indian style of cooking; meat marinated in yogurt and spices

tempura: meats or vegetables fried in a light batter and eaten with dipping sauce

tsukune: Japanese-style meatball, often grilled

umeboshi: pickled plums; available in a variety of sizes and textures

usuyaki tamago: Japanese-style crepe omelet, also called egg sheets; great for coloring

yukari: dried and seasoned red shiso leaves; used to create *ume shiso onigiri*

Metric Conversions

Volume

U.S.	Metric
¼ tsp	1.25 ml (cc)
½ tsp	2.5 ml (cc)
1 tsp	5 ml (cc)
1 tbsp (3 tsp)	15 ml (cc)
1 fl oz (2 tbsp)	30 ml (cc)
¼ cup	60 ml (cc)
⅓ cup	80 ml (cc)
½ cup	120 ml (cc)
1 cup	240 ml (cc)
1 pint (2 cups)	480 ml (cc)
1 quart (2 pints)	960 ml (cc)
1 gallon (4 quarts)	3.84 liters

Weight

U.S.	Metric
1 oz	28 g
4 oz (¼ lb)	113 g
8 oz (½ lb)	227 g
12 oz (¾ lb)	340 g
16 oz (1 lb)	454 g
2.2 lb	1 kg

Length

Inches	Centimeters
¼	0.65
½	1.25
1	2.50
2	5.00
3	7.50
4	10.0
5	12.5
6	15.0

Oven Temperature

Degrees Fahrenheit	Degrees Centigrade	British Gas Marks
200	93	—
250	120	½
275	140	1
300	150	2
325	165	3
350	175	4
375	190	5
400	200	6
450	230	8

Index

Acknowledgments

I'm deeply grateful to my sons, Kai and Hal, for giving me the chance to make bentos. To my husband, Yo, thank you very much for 20 years. You always watch with such affection, and I really appreciate all you've done for me. For my father, you gave me a special knife for cooking when I got married. To my mom, I still remember the bento you made for me when I was a girl. You taught me so much.

To Tiffany and the staff at Quirk, thank you from the bottom of my heart.

To Pikko, thank you for all your support and encouragement. I really appreciate all you've done for me.

I'm very grateful to all of our readers waiting for us to create this next book.

—Maki

First I'd like to thank my husband, Randall, for kindly putting up with my bento junkyard, which has silently grown over the years, and for occasionally publicly expressing uncharacteristic moments of pride regarding my work. This means more to me than any direct compliment. To my two older children, Kami and Brandon, who are my staunchest fans and critics, thank you for the encouragement and requests. To my youngest, Chase, who will be my little in-house guinea pig in the years to come, thank you for patiently (and sometimes not-so-patiently) watching me with interest from below.

To my mother, Jan, thank you for infecting me with your desire to bring your A-game when it came to food. To my mother-in-law, June, thank you for the endless support and yummy meals over the years. To my Grandma Mu, whom I still think of anytime I pull a pot out of the cupboard or stop myself from closing a fridge drawer with my foot. To my dad, Richard, thank you for teaching me about hard work by example. To my father-in-law, Jeff, thank you for always being willing to be there to help. To my brother, Nick, who can always make me laugh when I need it.

To Maki, I couldn't have asked for a more generous and talented bento partner. It's been a pleasure working with you again and I look forward to when we meet again.

To the staff at Quirk, thank you so much for giving Maki and me the chance to make another book. Last but not least, thank you to our readers. We hope you enjoy this book as much as the last one.

—Pikko

Bye for meow!